MULTIPLE CASUALTY INCIDENT

by Sami Ibrahim

Multiple Casualty Incident was first performed at The Yard Theatre, London, on 27 April 2024.

MULTIPLE CASUALTY INCIDENT

by Sami Ibrahim

CAST
Luca Kamleh Chapman | Khaled
Mariah Louca | Nicki
Peter Corboy | Dan
Rosa Robson | Sarah

CREATIVE AND PRODUCTION TEAM
Jaz Woodcock-Stewart | Director
Sami Ibrahim | Writer
Rosie Elnile | Set Designer
Tomás Palmer | Costume Designer
Zeynep Kepekli | Lighting Designer
Josh Anio Grigg | Sound Designer
Hamza Arnaout | Associate Sound Designer
Andrew Crofts | Video Designer
Raniah Al-Sayed | Intimacy Coordinator
Jatinder Chera | Casting Director
Aaron Kilercioglu | Assistant Director
Isabelle Cook | Costume Supervisor
Marina Ambrosone | Costume Placement
James Dawson | Production Manager
Julia Nimmo | Company Stage Manager
Rhea Cosford | Assistant Stage Manager

BIOGRAPHIES

Luca Kamleh Chapman
Luca Kamleh Chapman plays Khaled. He graduated from Oxford
School of Drama.

Theatre credits include *The EU Killed My Dad* (Jermyn Street
Theatre); *Grey Rock* (Remote Theatre Project); *two
Palestinians go dogging* (Royal Court).

Theatre credits at Oxford School of Drama include *A Lie of
the Mind*, *As You Like It*, *Medea* and *A Couple of Poor, Polish-
Speaking Romanians.*

Film credits include *Anna* (Good Films Collective); *How To
Have Sex* (Film4 & BFI).

TV credits include *The Gathering* (Channel 4/World
Productions).

Mariah Louca
Mariah Louca plays Nicki.

Mariah's theatre credits include *The Doctor* (Almeida/Adelaide
Festival/UK tour/Duke of York's/Park Avenue Armory, New York);
Burnt at the Stake, or The Whole of the Truth (Shakespeare's
Globe); *Best of Enemies* (Young Vic/Noël Coward); *Maryland*
(Royal Court/Battersea Arts Centre); *Queer Upstairs* (Royal
Court); *The Ministry of Lesbian Affairs* (Soho); *Cherry Jezebel*
(Liverpool Everyman); *All Mod Cons* (Lyric, Belfast); *Julius
Caesar*, *Playing for Time*, *A Dream*, *The Sheffield Mysteries* and
20 Tiny Plays About Sheffield (Sheffield Crucible); *Ajar*
(Theatre By The Lake/Graeae); *Tuesdays at Tesco's* and *Bloom,
Blossom, Bloom* (Southwark Playhouse); *Bumps* (Theatre503); *The
Interview* (The Mono Box/PLAYSTART) and *The Vagina Monologues*
(Theatre Delicatessen).

Film credits include *Jingle Bell Heist* and *Re-Displacement*
(short).

On TV, Mariah has appeared in *Waterloo Road*, *EastEnders*,
Casualty and *Doctors* (BBC).

Peter Corboy
Peter Corboy plays Dan. He trained at Trinity College Dublin
and the Royal Welsh College of Music and Drama.

Recent theatre credits include *Ulysses* (Jermyn Street
Theatre); *Hothouse*, *Before You Say Anything* and *Everything
Not Saved* (MALAPROP).

Film credits include *Flora & Son* (Apple TV).

TV credits include *The Vanishing Triangle* (AMC+, Virgin
Media) and *Fair City* (RTÉ), and he just wrapped filming on
a series for Apple TV+.

Rosa Robson
Rosa Robson plays Sarah. Rosa studied at Cambridge University and whilst there was a member of the Cambridge Footlights, with whom she toured the UK and internationally.

Her stage credits include a season at the RSC in 2016; *Don Quixote* (Barbican); *Here Are The Ghosts* (Royal Court) and *A Table Tennis Play* (Edinburgh Fringe Festival).

For screen, Rosa is known for her roles in Season 2 of *Extraordinary* (Disney); *Big Boys* (Channel 4); *Buffering* (ITV); *Inside No. 9* (BBC) and the BIFA-winning film *Black Mountain Poets* (Film4).

Jaz Woodcock-Stewart
Jaz Woodcock-Stewart is a director working in theatre and performance. She was nominated for an Olivier Award last year for her production of *Paradise Now!* at the Bush Theatre. Her play *Civilisation* won the Jury Prize at Fast Forward, the European Festival for Young Stage Directors at Dresden Staatsschauspiel. She was also nominated by the National Theatre to create *Something New* at Performance Laboratory Salzburg 2019. She is the Artistic Director of award-winning arts company, Antler, Associate Company at the Bush Theatre 2017-18. Jaz is an associate artist at Brixton House.

As Director, Jaz's productions include *Jason Medea Medley* (Staatsschauspiel Dresden); *Paradise Now!, Lands* (Bush); *Electric Rosary* (Royal Exchange); *Gulliver's Travels* (Unicorn); *Civilisation* (New Diorama/HOME Manchester/ Hellerau); *Madrigal* (RCSSD); *Fen* (Lamda); *Learning Piece* (The Place); *Something New* (Performance Laboratory Salzburg, Thomas Bernhard Institut/NT/Mitos21); *Mother Courage, The Bacchae* (East 15 Acting School); *Wifmon* (National Theatre Studio) and *If I Were Me* (Underbelly/Bush/Soho).

Sami Ibrahim
Writer Sami Ibrahim won Theatre Uncut's Political Playwriting Award for *two Palestinians go dogging*, which ran at the Royal Court in 2023 and was nominated for an Olivier Award for 'Outstanding Achievement in an Affiliate Theatre'. He has been on attachment at the National Theatre Studio and writer-in-residence at Shakespeare's Globe – where he co-wrote *Metamorphoses*, which was performed in 2021 and recently transferred to the Seattle Rep in Washington. He is working on a handful of theatre commissions and developing a feature film with BBC Film and A24-backed company 2am.

Sami's theatre credits include *A Sudden Violent Burst of Rain* (Paines Plough/Gate); *two Palestinians go dogging* (Royal Court/Theatre Uncut); *Metamorphoses* (Shakespeare's Globe); *Wonder Winterland* (Oxford School of Drama/Soho); *the Palestinian in the basement is on fire* (Pint-Sized/The Bunker); *Wind Bit Bitter, Bit Bit Bit Her* (VAULT Festival); *Iron Dome Fog Dome* (The Yard Theatre/First Drafts); *Carnivore* (Brockley Jack). Audio credits include *50 Berkeley Square* and *Fledgling* (Radio 4) and *The Twig* (That Podcast ETT).

Rosie Elnile
Rosie Elnile is an award-winning performance designer. She was a recipient of the Jerwood Live Work Fund 2020 and was an associate artist of The Gate Theatre.

For The Yard Theatre: *The Cherry Orchard*, *An unfinished man* and *Big Guns*.

Other design credits include *Faggots and Their Friends Between The Revolutions* (Manchester International Festival and Festival d'Aix en Provance); *Jason Medea Medley* (Staatsschauspiel, Dresden); *Titus Andronicus* (Shakespeare's Globe); *Sound of the Underground*, *A Fight Against...* (Una Lucha Contra...); *Goats* and *Primetime 2017* (Royal Court); *Paradise Now!* (Bush); *Violet* (Britten Pears Art; co-pro with Royal Opera and Music Theatre Wales); *Peaceophobia* (Fuel Theatre); *Prayer*, *The Ridiculous Darkness*, *The Unknown Island* and *The Convert* (Gate); *Thirst Trap* (Fuel); *Run Sister Run* (Crucible); *[Blank]* (Donmar Warehouse); *Our Town* (Regent's Park Open Air Theatre); *The Wolves* (Theatre Royal Stratford East); *The Mysteries* and *Three Sisters* (Royal Exchange); *Abandon* (Lyric Hammersmith) and *Returning to Haifa* (Finborough).

Tomás Palmer
Tomás Palmer is an artist and designer who works across theatre, dance, opera and performance art. Tomás trained at the Glasgow School of Art and the Royal Welsh College of Music and Drama. He was the production designer on the BAFTA and BIFA Award-winning short film *Too Rough* in 2022.

As an artist, he has created installations/performance pieces for the Centre for Contemporary Arts (Glasgow), Transmission Gallery (Glasgow) and Embassy Gallery (Edinburgh).

Set and costume design credits include *Blue Mist* (Royal Court); *The Bacchae* (The Lyric Hammersmith); *My Uncle Is Not Pablo Escobar* (Brixton House); *Sanctuary* (Access All Areas); *Sophocles' Oedipus / Silent Practice* (LAMDA); *The Wellspring* (co-design with Rosie Elnile; Royal & Derngate, Northampton); *Time Is Running Out* (Gate, Cardiff); *Winning* (Glasgow School of Art) and *Autocue* (Centre for Contemporary Art Glasgow).

Costume design credits include *Julius Caesar* (co-costume design with Rosanna Vize; RSC).

Zeynep Kepekli

Zeynep Kepekli is a London-based lighting designer who creates work around the world across dance, theatre, opera, ballet, site-specific projects, and installations.

She trained in art and her work is influenced by nature, architecture and bodies in spaces. She is particularly interested in researching natural light and its transformative effects on the land. She continuously questions geography and belonging in her work.

Some of her recent credits include *Festival of New Choreography* (Royal Ballet; The Royal Opera House); *California Connections* (Yorke Dance Project; The Royal Opera House); *Common Grounds* (Pina Bausch Foundation/École de Sables/Sadler's Wells); *The Meaning of Zong* (Tom Morris/Giles Terera; Bristol Old Vic) and *How Did We Get Here?* (Julie Cunningham Co + Mel C; Sadler's Wells).

Josh Anio Grigg

Josh Anio Grigg is a sound designer and multimedia artist living in London, UK. He often works on the creation of theatre, dance and art installations.

His work for The Yard Theatre includes *The Flea*, *Dirty Crusty*, *The Crucible*, *A New & Better You*, *This Beautiful Future*, *Removal Men*, *Made Visible*, *Mikvah Project* and *Beyond Caring.*

His recent works include *The Confessions* (Volkstheater/ National Theatre/La FabricA, Avignon); *IV* (SERAFINE1369; The Yard Theatre); *Inchoate Buzz* (Tramway, Glasgow, 202); *Love* (Park Avenue Armory, New York) and *Live to Tell* (Camden People's Theatre).

Josh is interested in lots of technologies — linking together digital, light, audio, video and performance ideas. His enthusiasm across disciplines helps him to think creatively about how production techniques overlap and interlock in useful and exciting ways. He regularly works supporting artists and projects, researching and developing new ideas and how to achieve them with accessible and robust techniques.

Hamza Arnaout

Hamza Arnaout, also known as El Jehaz, is a talented Jordanian guitarist who has been involved with two popular Middle Eastern bands: Autostrad and 47soul. He joined Autostrad in 2008, and with his guitar playing, he contributed to the band's unique fusion of Arabic and Western music. With Autostrad, he released several albums and gained a large following in the Middle East and Europe.

In 2013, Arnaout co-founded 47soul, a band known for their fusion of traditional Palestinian music, electronic beats, and hip-hop influences. Through his involvement with both bands, Arnaout has become a prominent figure in the Middle Eastern music scene, known for his innovative guitar playing and contribution to the fusion of traditional and modern music in the SWANA region.

Andrew Crofts

Andrew Crofts is a lighting and video designer with a background in live art and contemporary performance. Since 2005 he has worked extensively with the groundbreaking company imitating the dog, as well as more widely across theatre, dance and opera with companies and artists such as Jasmin Vardimon Company, Nigel and Louise, Keisha Thompson and Blast Theory.

Raniah Al-Sayed

Raniah Al-Sayed is a movement practitioner and intimacy director, specialising in the physical acting process of Lucid Body. She is a faculty member at Shakespeare's Globe Higher Education Department and continues to teach through her company Lucid Body London.

Intimacy director credits include *Peaky Blinders: The Rise* (Immersive Everywhere); *Bootycandy* (The Gate); *£1 Thursdays* (Finborough); *Supernova* (Theatre503); *How a City Can Save the World*, *The Hypochondriac* and *Fossil Kids* (Sheffield People's Theatre); *Machinal* (Intimacy Consultant/CSSD); *Follies* (CSSD); *Earthquakes* (ALRA); *The Welkin* (Conti Arts); *A Start Next to the Moon* (Guildhall Opera); *Days of Significance*, *Attempts on Her Life*, *The Gift*, *Our Town*, *Hyde & Seek*, *Dennis of Penge*, *Intimate Apparel*, *Road* and *Pilgrims* (GSMD).

Intimacy coordinator credits for film/TV include *I'm Not Finished* (dir. Rebecca Gausnell); *The Wife and Her House Husband* (dir. Marcus Markou); *Salt Wounds* (dir. Hannah Renton); *Remi Milligan: Lost Director* (dir. Samuel Lodato); *Break the Rule* (LCC, dir. Beata Jamroziak); Asst I.C. on *Dreamland* (Merman Prods, dir. Ellie Heydon).

Assistant Director credits include *A Voice Lesson: Orla Descends* (Britten Pears Arts).

Future plans include *Alize's Room* (dir. Anna Fearon) and *Jane Eyre* (Guildhall School of Music & Drama).

Jatinder Chera

Jatinder Chera took a position at the National Theatre, following his graduation from the Casting Certificate, at the National Film and Television School. Prior to this, he worked as an actor, having trained at Millennium Performing Arts.

For The Yard Theatre, Jatinder cast *The Flea* and *Samuel Takes a Break*. Further credits include *The Comeuppance* (Almeida); Olivier Award-winning *The P Word*, *A Playlist for the Revolution*, *Sleepova* (Bush); *Sweat* (Royal Exchange); *The Nutcracker* (Bristol Old Vic); *Up Next Gala 2022* (Lyttelton auditorium, National Theatre) and *A Family Business* (Staatstheater Mainz/UK tour).

As Casting Associate at the National Theatre, he worked on: *The Father and the Assassin* (Olivier Theatre).

As Casting Assistant at the National Theatre, Jatinder worked on *Othello* and *Much Ado About Nothing* (Lyttelton Theatre), *Small Island* (Olivier Theatre), and *Trouble in Mind* (Dorfman Theatre).

Aaron Kilercioglu

Aaron Kilercioglu is a writer and director whose latest play *The EU Killed My Dad* won the Woven Voices Prize and was nominated for two Offies, including Best Production. He's currently working on a handful of theatre commissions, including for Eleanor Lloyd Company, and Zorlu PSM, Istanbul, as well as developing a feature film for Karga7. His work has won the Untapped Award, the BOLD Playwrights Prize and has been shortlisted for the Theatre503 International Playwriting Prize. He's been a member of Old Vic Playwriting, Bush Theatre Emerging Writers, Royal Court Young Agitators, and the London Library Emerging Writers Programme.

Aaron's theatre credits include *The EU Killed My Dad* (Woven Voices/Jermyn Street); *For a Palestinian* (Bristol Old Vic/ Camden People's Theatre); *A Guest* (VAULT Festival) and *CICADA 3301* (Underbelly).

Isabelle Cook

For theatre, Isabelle Cook has worked as a costume supervisor on *The Odyssey* (Unicorn) and *Blue Mist* (Royal Court).

For film and television she has worked as a design assistant/ Buyer on *Queen Charlotte: A Bridgerton Story*, a crowd costume assistant on *Gangs of London*, a principal standby on *Mary and George* and a costume designer on *Hermit, Measure, Sensory Prosthetics, In Vitro.*

As Key Crowd for film, Isabelle worked on *People We Hate at the Wedding.* As Crowd Standby for film, Isabelle worked on *The Three-Body Problem*, *I Hate Suzie*, *Ted Lasso*, *SAS Rogue Heroes*, *Damsel*, *Snow White* and *Bridgerton.*

Marina Ambrosone

Marina Ambrosone is a costume supervisor, maker, wardrobe assistant and buyer, currently training at RADA on a Postgraduate Diploma in Theatre Costume.

Some of her recent credits include Associate Costume Designer and Supervisor for *The War of the Roses* (Shakespeare's Globe Youth Company).

Whilst training, costume supervisor credits include *Mirandolina* (dir. Simona Gonella); *Love & Information* (dir. Tim Hoare) and *Romeo and Juliet* (Shakespeare for Young Audiences, dir. Darren Raymond).

James Dawson
James Dawson is a freelance production manager for theatre,
opera and dance. Working across London, nationally and
internationally with a passion for touring work, performance
art and community projects. Consistently working across
a wide range of projects such as interactive children's play
spaces: REPLAY @ Southbank Centre; the co-production with
Headlong on A View from the Bridge; young and community-based
performances at Birmingham Rep (Order & Chaos) and global
touring with performer, Marikiscrycrycry, GONER. James has
worked at/with IF Opera, Young Vic Theatre, Unicorn Theatre,
National Youth Theatre, Chichester Festival Theatre and The
Yard Theatre.

Julia Nimmo
Julia Nimmo trained in Design for Theatre & Television at
Charles Stuart University, Wagga Wagga, Australia and was
awarded Individual Stage Manager of the Year at the SMA
National Stage Manager Awards 2019.

Stage manager theatre credits include Recognition (Talawa
Theatre Company); A Proper Ordinary Miracle (National Theatre
Wales); A Midsummer Night's Dream and The Tempest (Guildford
Shakespeare Company); An unfinished man (The Yard Theatre);
Run It Back (Talawa Theatre Company); Buffering… (Palace
Youth Company, Watford Palace Theatre); Queer Lives
(Historical Royal Palaces, Tower of London); Rust and The
Trick (HighTide/Bush); Songlines (HighTide/Dugout); Paper.
Scissors. Stone. (Tara Finney Productions); Frankie Vah (Paul
Jellis Ltd); All the Things I Lied About (Paul Jellis Ltd/
Katie Bonna); Harrogate (HighTide/Royal Court); This Much
(Moving Dust); Flare Path (Birdsong Productions/Original);
Lampedusa (HighTide/Soho); Beached (Marlowe/Soho); The One
(Soho); The Real Thing (English Touring Theatre); Macbeth
(Wildfire Productions, Cell Block Theatre, Sydney) and The
Beauty Queen of Leenane (Wildfire Productions, Seymour
Centre, Sydney).

Rhea Cosford
Rhea Cosford studied Drama at Queen Mary University of London
before going on to train in Stage and Events Management at
the Royal Welsh College of Music and Drama.

Stage management theatre credits include 2:22: A Ghost Story
(Runaway Entertainment/The Criterion); Trade (ELMA Productions/
The Pleasance); Walk Right Back and The Everly Brothers Story
(Grayne Productions/UK tour); Phantasmagoria (Kali/Southwark
Playhouse) and What Would Jarvis Do? (Omnibus).

'The Yard Theatre is a mecca for some of the most interesting theatre in Britain.' *British Vogue*

The Yard reimagines theatre. Our programme crosses genres and breaks boundaries, because the artists we work with want to say something new, in new ways. We work with artists who reflect the diversity of East London, who tell new stories. They invite us into journeys of escape, euphoria, possibility and hope. Through this, The Yard reimagines the world.

We've developed artists like Michaela Coel, Alexander Zeldin, Marikiscrycrycry and Dipo Baruwa-Etti, Yard Young Artists like Lamesha Ruddock and nightlife collectives like INFERNO and Pxssy Palace. They've all used their vision and energy to give us new stories and narratives for what the world could be.

Recent work includes: ★★★★★ *Samuel Takes a Break* written by Rhianna Ilube, directed by Anthony Simpson-Pike (2024), ★★★★★ *The Flea* written by James Fritz, directed by Jay Miller (2023), ★★★★★ *An unfinished man* written by Dipo Baruwa-Etti, directed by Taio Lawson (2022), *The Cherry Orchard*, reimagined by Vinay Patel, directed by James Macdonald (2022), ★★★★★ *The Crucible* written by Arthur Miller, directed by Jay Miller (2019), ★★★★★ *Dirty Crusty* written by Clare Barron, directed by Jay Miller (2019), ★★★★ *Armadillo* written by Sarah Kosar, directed by Sara Joyce (2020), ★★★★ *A New and Better You* by Joe Harbot, directed by Cheryl Gallacher (2018) and ★★★★★ *Buggy Baby* by Josh Azouz, directed by Ned Bennett (2018).

theyardtheatre.co.uk
@theyardtheatre

MULTIPLE CASUALTY INCIDENT

Sami Ibrahim

Characters

DAN, *thirty*
KHALED, *twenty-five*
NICKI, *thirty-nine*
SARAH, *thirty-three*

Time

Some time close to the present.

Setting

A training centre in London.

Notes

A dash (–) indicates an active pause.

Sentences without a full stop are unfinished or interrupted.

Accents should probably be avoided.

After the performance, the audience might be given the option
to donate to a chosen charity.

*This text went to press before the end of rehearsals and so may
differ slightly from the play as performed.*

An under-decorated room: stark and white. A few chairs are stacked to one side, there's a rubbish bin, scraps of paper that haven't made it in, a kettle and mugs on the floor in the corner, a duffel bag filled with clothes, a backpack, and whatever else you'd find in an empty room.

Stage left there are some double doors leading into the hallway.

Stage right, an emergency fire exit.

NICKI *sits in a chair up against the back wall.*

Next to her, but not too close, is KHALED.

NICKI   I can get you a tea or a coffee or...

KHALED   I'm good.
                 Thanks.

              Pause.

NICKI   They should've told me last week.

KHALED   It's no problem.

NICKI   Well I'm sorry.
                 About that.

              Another pause.

              I wanted to say there's a world where you take time off.

KHALED   I don't need time off.

NICKI   Okay.

              And another pause.

              NICKI *checks her watch.*

              I'm just trying to think of
              Before they get here

KHALED   –

NICKI   As in it's not the same this week, you know, you've
           got to be up for throwing yourself in, trying stuff out.

KHALED   I get that.

NICKI   Which is great.

KHALED   And I'm doing fine, I don't need people sticking
           their nose in.

NICKI   No one's sticking their nose in, it's

           Then NICKI*'s phone goes off. She rejects the call.*

KHALED   You can take it, I don't mind.

NICKI   It can wait.

KHALED   –

NICKI   Look, I'm not trying to tell you what to do but
           I think
           The more people you have around to…
           You know, the easier it'll be.
           And obviously that can be difficult.

KHALED   Difficult?

NICKI   Sometimes. But maybe you could do with, I don't
           know

           Her phone goes off again. She sighs.

           You know what, is that alright?

           NICKI *stands, answers her phone –*

           Hey. Yeah, uh-huh, look. I'm about to

           – and leaves the room.

           KHALED *waits. For a moment. Then he stands.*
           He unstacks a couple of chairs.

           SARAH *enters.*

SARAH   Hey.

KHALED   Hi.

She puts her bag in the corner of the room.

SARAH   Good weekend?

KHALED   Fine.

SARAH   Get up to anything?

KHALED   Not much. You?

SARAH   Not much either.

                An awkward pause.

KHALED   Um. I'm just gonna

                KHALED *drags a chair over to the centre of the room, places it there.* SARAH *picks up a chair and puts it next to the first chair.*

                DAN *enters.*

DAN   All good all good?

SARAH   Morning.

DAN   Everyone else have a shit weekend?

                DAN *dumps his bag and helps move a chair too.*

                I spent a whole Saturday getting a verruca burnt off my foot. I couldn't get a proper view but they sort of boil it with this needle thing and then scoop it out, sort of looks like a child's tooth covered in blood. My advice would be never get a fucking verruca, they might as well have stuck my foot in acid, I don't know why they don't give you anaesthetic. Honestly, I spent Sunday limping up to the big Asda and back, some guy dropped fifty p in my coffee cup cos he thought I was homeless.
                Hey man.

KHALED   Hey.

DAN   My foot's fine now.
                Where is she?

KHALED   Taking a call.

By now, five chairs have been set up in a sort of semicircle in the centre of the room.

It's quiet.

DAN *checks his phone,* SARAH *goes over to her bag,* KHALED *takes a seat.*

Finally, NICKI *comes back in.*

NICKI   Right, sorry, I'm in the room – how's everyone doing?

NICKI gets a mumbled response as she goes over to her bag, gets out some sheets.

Who's got the time?

SARAH   Almost ten.

NICKI   Perfecto. So we should start with

But NICKI notices not everyone is there.

Ah. Has anyone heard from her?

SARAH   Not since Friday.

NICKI   Okay, um

DAN   Should someone message her?

NICKI   No. That's fine. She'll have to catch up.

                              *

SARAH   Act, react, reflect.

DAN   Someone's done the homework.

NICKI   We do it, we get it wrong, we discuss. Dan.

The group is sat in a circle.

DAN   What?

NICKI   The point is to engage, there are no right answers.

DAN   Just stupid answers.

NICKI   And if you give a stupid answer then we do it again. And again. And again because when you're in the middle of it all, this has to be clockwork,

there's no figuring things out.
Especially where you'll be.
Especially now.

A beat.

Let's start with an exercise.

*

KHALED *looks at his phone.* SARAH *drinks a cup of tea.* NICKI *flicks through some papers.*

DAN *fiddles with the kettle – maybe he flicks it on and off.*

DAN   What time are we back?

Pause. No reply.

Hello?

NICKI   Ten minutes.

DAN   Ten minutes. Does anyone have a phone charger?

*

SARAH   I would tell the patient directly.

NICKI   She has dementia, she struggles to understand.

SARAH   I would still use the translator, I would make it clear.

NICKI   And if her son's trying to find out what's happening.

SARAH   It's meant to stay confidential.

NICKI   But if she's not listening, if it needs to happen now.

SARAH   I'd still use the translator.

NICKI   If she refuses.

SARAH   Then I'd ask her if I can tell the son.

NICKI   If he refuses.

SARAH   He wouldn't.

NICKI   He doesn't want his mum's leg being sawn off.

SARAH   I would explain the situation clearly and

NICKI   And if he's shouting and his mother is scared and wailing and you need the leg to be removed before an infection spreads, how are you making them listen?

           Now SARAH *hesitates. The rest of the group waits for an answer.*

           Sarah?

                              *

           SARAH *is rooting through her bag.* KHALED *is eating a sandwich.* DAN *is sitting in the corner, eating a banana.*

SARAH   Shit.

DAN   You alright?

SARAH   I make a sandwich every day, every day I forget it.

           SARAH *stands, walks over to the double doors.*

           Anyone need anything from the shop?

KHALED   Have this half.

SARAH   Oh. Really?

KHALED   Yeah.

SARAH   What about you?

KHALED   I'm not too hungry.

           KHALED *holds out half a sandwich.*

           Ploughman's no mayo. Fell on the floor but otherwise it's fine.

           SARAH *takes the half sandwich from* KHALED.

SARAH   Thanks.

DAN   I've got crisps.

SARAH   It's alright.

DAN   Always carry a spare Monster Munch.

SARAH   I'm good. Cheers.

DAN   Suit yourself.

SARAH sits next to KHALED.

SARAH   I owe you one.

KHALED Nah, don't worry.

They eat together, in silence.

SARAH   It's, um, it's delicious.

KHALED Tesco Meal Deal.

SARAH   You can tell – very gourmet.

KHALED *laughs.*

Sorry, that's such a dorky joke.

KHALED I like a dorky joke.

They continue eating, in silence. DAN *stands –*

DAN   I need a piss.

– and he walks out. Pause.

KHALED Did that make you lose your appetite too?

SARAH *smiles.*

SARAH	Um, actually	KHALED	So um
	I was gonna		Oh.
	Sorry.		It's fine.
	No.		
	You go.		

They continue eating.

KHALED No, you go.

Pause.

SARAH   I just didn't know if… like I thought I might get a text. From you.

KHALED Oh.

SARAH   Not that you had to.

KHALED   I would've but

SARAH   It's really fine.

          Pause.

KHALED   I meant to but I didn't really know if you actually
          wanted me to or

SARAH   I did.

KHALED   Right.

SARAH   Cos it might've been nice. If you weren't up to
          much.

KHALED   Yeah.

SARAH   Maybe next time.

                              *

NICKI   Her father's refusing entry.

          A beat. The group watches NICKI *and* KHALED.

          She's fourteen, she's pregnant, you're pretty sure
          it's the father who's

KHALED   I know.

NICKI   So are you reporting it?

KHALED   After I speak to the father.

NICKI   He's not letting her out of the tent, he's not letting
          you examine her.

KHALED   And I'd have a woman with me for starters.

NICKI   He refuses to speak to a female.

KHALED   She can speak to the daughter.

NICKI   He won't let you speak to the daughter.

KHALED   –

NICKI   Are you focusing on the act of abuse or the health
          of the child?

KHALED   –

NICKI   How are you getting her out of the tent?

KHALED   Sorry but I'm a fucking nurse, no one's asking me
           to coax pregnant teenagers out of tents.

NICKI   It's a scenario.

KHALED   It's
           okay.
           Sorry.

NICKI   If it's too much, we'll discuss as a group.

KHALED   I'm fine, I can keep going.

NICKI   It's okay not to have answers.

KHALED   No, I'm good.

NICKI   –

KHALED   Honestly, I am good.

NICKI   –

KHALED   I would confront him about the abuse.

                         *

           SARAH *and* DAN *are alone in the room.*

DAN   She's still not here.

SARAH   Yeah.

DAN   See I reckon she quit.

           DAN *turns on the kettle.* SARAH *watches him.*

SARAH   I mean, odds are she's ill.

DAN   She quit.

SARAH   Or, like, she needed a break.

DAN   She quit.
           Cup of tea?

SARAH   I'm fine.
           Why would she walk out?

DAN   That's what I'm saying cos I know her and she tells
           me stuff but clearly she didn't so something's
           happened.

SARAH   Maybe you don't know her as well as you think.

DAN   I know her.

SARAH   She applied like four times.

DAN   So what?

SARAH   So she wouldn't.

DAN   Okay.

           DAN *puts a teabag in a mug, waits for the kettle
           to boil.*

SARAH   I just don't think she's that selfish.

DAN   No?

SARAH   No.

DAN   Even when she was eyeing up other jobs last week.

SARAH   You think she took one?

DAN   Maybe.

SARAH   So she got this and then she thought – *nah fuck
           that, I'm off somewhere else.*

DAN   Maybe she couldn't hack it.

SARAH   But that's the point.
           That's why we're here.
           Not giving up when there's a complete mess
           waiting for us.

DAN   I know.

           The kettle boils and DAN *pours himself a tea.*
           KHALED *enters, a bag on his shoulder.*

           We reckon Lisa quit.

KHALED   Huh?

DAN   What do you think?

KHALED   Well she's obviously not ill.

SARAH   Why not?

KHALED   She said she was scared of what's happening out there.

*

NICKI   It's always worse than you think.

A beat. The group is sat around, silent.

And you'll be in at the start of a mission, mistakes get made, it's chaos, but don't forget it can always get worse.
You could be on two hours' sleep, Saturday night, everyone's coming in drunk, everyone's fighting, it gets worse.
A&E after a motorway pile-up, it gets worse.
You watch the news, listen to your podcasts, it gets worse.
You could've been out there for years and, I promise, there's still a day waiting for you that's worse.
Always.

DAN   What's the point of this then?

SARAH   Cos she just said, it always gets worse.

*

KHALED eats a sandwich and flicks through his phone.

DAN eats a pack of crisps and flicks through his phone.

Then DAN goes over to the kettle, checks if there's enough water in it. He's about to turn it on when KHALED sighs.

The two look at each other.

Then KHALED goes back to looking at his phone.

DAN hovers for a moment.

DAN   Hey, um

KHALED   –

DAN   Are you looking at all this about another…

KHALED   Uh-huh.

A beat.

DAN   Shit, isn't it?

KHALED   –

DAN   Are you doing alright?

KHALED   Me?

DAN   I mean
If you've got family out there, are they…

KHALED   Different part of the country.

DAN   Oh. Right. Still.

KHALED   It happens a lot.

DAN   What, a hundred people happens a lot? In one attack?

KHALED   –

DAN   Sorry, I'm not trying to… I just can't imagine having family so close.

KHALED   Where's your family from?

DAN   Um. Why?

KHALED   Cos if someone sets off a bomb in, I dunno, Norwich, am I gonna ask if you're alright?

DAN   Only if you thought Norwich was in Ireland.

Pause.

Look, do you want a cup of tea?

KHALED   Nah, I could do with some air actually.

*

DAN   So.
           Yes.
           I guess I'm the first one in the Multiple Casualty
           Incident.
           I'm, um, a male.
           Aged eighteen.
           I am conscious.
           My breath is shallow.
           High pulse.

           DAN holds an index card and checks it briefly.

           *The rest of the group is stood around, chairs
           pushed to the side.*

NICKI   Do you have a name?

DAN   Oh.

NICKI   I feel like we should give you a name if we're
           about to save your life.

DAN   –

NICKI   Anyone?

KHALED   Ali?

NICKI   Ali.
           We like Ali.
           Tell us more about Ali.

           A beat.

DAN   So Ali is

NICKI   You are

DAN   I am
           struggling to breathe
           high pulse
           screaming very loudly.
           I've been brought in on a stretcher and have an
           open wound on my left upper arm.
           It might be fractured but
           It's obviously very painful, caused by a bullet, but
           the bullet is no longer lodged in the muscle.

NICKI   Triage?

DAN   I'm losing quite a lot of blood but
               I'm young, you'd probably stabilise me without
               much effort so
               Yeah, I'd go close to the top.

NICKI   Do we all agree?

                                    *

SARAH   'A vulnerable patient with a history of trauma,
               self-harm and suicidal ideation has come into your
               medical centre. After examination, you discover
               that the patient has a wound which is infected and
               their prognosis is poor. This news is likely to
               trigger their behavioural history. Do you or do you
               not deliver the prognosis?'

               SARAH *finishes reading from the card*, KHALED
               is opposite.

               Towards the back of the room, NICKI *and* DAN
               are chatting.

KHALED   That's all it gives us?

SARAH   Yup.

KHALED   Nothing else?

SARAH   Nope.

               Pause.

KHALED   I hate these things.

SARAH   Me too.

               Pause.

KHALED   No.

SARAH   What?

KHALED   I wouldn't tell him. Done.

               Pause. SARAH *laughs.*

SARAH   She said we're meant to use examples.

KHALED   Doesn't matter, I wouldn't tell him.

SARAH   You're meant to take it seriously.

KHALED   I am!

SARAH   –

KHALED   Go on then, pick an example.

SARAH   Okay. Ali.

KHALED   Ali.

SARAH   With the bullet wound.

KHALED   Ali with the bullet wound – and, what, now it's
            infected?

SARAH   According to this.

KHALED   And also he's got a history of trauma?

SARAH   Uh-huh.

KHALED   And self-harm?

SARAH   Uh-huh.

KHALED   And he's, what, eighteen?

SARAH   The kid's seen a lot.

            A beat.

            Go on then, what are we gonna do with poor
            vulnerable Ali?

KHALED   You mean trauma-ridden Ali.

SARAH   Refugee Ali.

KHALED   Primary-Actor Ali.

SARAH   Suicidal-ideation Ali.

KHALED   That's bad.

SARAH   You're laughing.

KHALED   I'm not.

SARAH   You are.

KHALED   You said it.

NICKI *looks up from speaking with* DAN.

NICKI   One more minute and I want to discuss.

SARAH   Okay.
Bollocks.
Why don't we um

KHALED   What about family, is he with family?

SARAH   That's up to us.

KHALED   So say his family's there, tell them.

SARAH   But if they're not.

KHALED *sighs*.

Like, I dunno, say his dad's dead.

KHALED   Tell his mum.

SARAH   Khaled.

KHALED   –

SARAH   His dad's dead cos they
He got hit by a bullet.
It was a border crossing, wasn't it?
Primary Actors trying to cross, there's an attack,
chaos, maybe Ali got separated from his dad and
Yeah.
It happens.
Shot to the head.
Lots of blood.
Struggling to survive and Ali comes back later and
Dad dies in his arms.
The trauma.
And he's alone and he's wounded and now he's…
So what are we doing with him?

KHALED   –

SARAH   Khaled?

KHALED   –

SARAH   Khaled?

           Again NICKI *looks up, calls over.*

NICKI   Are we all done?

SARAH   You're meant to say something.

NICKI   Guys?

SARAH   Yeah, hold on, we're just
           Khaled?

           KHALED *still doesn't respond. Now* NICKI *is
           walking over.*

NICKI   What's going on?

                              *

           KHALED *and* SARAH *are alone.*

SARAH   I'm so sorry.

KHALED   –

SARAH   I know you didn't want people knowing but

KHALED   I don't need people screwing me around.

SARAH   No one's screwing you around, it just might help
           if we…

KHALED   –

SARAH   You shouldn't be embarrassed.

KHALED   What when I couldn't stop fucking crying,
           I shouldn't be embarrassed?

           Pause.

SARAH   If I'd known I wouldn't have…

KHALED   I'm good.

SARAH   Are you?

KHALED   –

SARAH   Look, when someone passes, it can be

KHALED   He didn't pass, he died.

SARAH   Right.

KHALED   People say *passed*, like they're being sensitive, like
          they're pretending it was all peaceful and somehow
          that's meant to help but
          He got ill, no one could do anything, he died.

SARAH   Khaled.

KHALED   And I swear, the number of cousins and aunts and
          uncles that turned up afterwards, not speaking a word
          of English, and me and Mum just sitting there in
          silence as they all shout and cry and laugh and eat
          and hug and

SARAH   It sounds like a lot of people were there to support
          you.

KHALED   I think it gets indulgent.

          Pause.

SARAH   You know, you're allowed to… like, you should be
          vulnerable, it's a good thing.

KHALED   I'm aware.

SARAH   Are you sure about that?

KHALED   –

SARAH   You're just here to do the training, is that it?

KHALED   Uh-huh.

SARAH   And that's fine but

KHALED   But what?

SARAH   –

KHALED   They already asked if I want time off, I've spent
          the last five months having time off.

SARAH takes a moment. Then goes to pick up her bag.

SARAH   Is it better if I leave you alone?

KHALED   Sarah.

SARAH   It's fine, I honestly don't mind.

KHALED   I'm just not very good at, like

SARAH   I said I don't mind.

Then SARAH heads to the door.

KHALED   Cos I was gonna, um

SARAH   You should get some rest. And you were great today but

KHALED   I wasn't.

SARAH   You were.

Pause. And maybe KHALED is about to say something but –

Look, I'll catch you tomorrow.

SARAH goes.

KHALED waits.

Then he kicks a chair over.

*

The group stands around as SARAH reads from an index card.

SARAH   'A Primary Actor, with whom you have a personal relationship, arrives at the medical centre with an open wound. You commence treatment but shouts and screams are soon heard from outside the facility. A colleague comes in to tell you that the facility is in danger of being attacked and a lack of security means your organisation can't keep everyone safe.

> Medical Provider One argues that you have a
> responsibility to continue providing care as normal.
> Medical Provider Two argues that care should
> cease until it is safe for all members of the
> organisation to continue working.'

NICKI   Thank you Sarah. Is that all clear?

SARAH   Yup.

NICKI   So if Sarah takes Medical Provider One.

SARAH   Great.

NICKI   Can I get a Medical Provider Two?

            KHALED *raises his hand*.

            How about Dan? Just for now.

            DAN *steps forward*.

            And no pausing, let's see what happens.

SARAH   Okay.

DAN   Sure.

            SARAH *and* DAN *are opposite each other, about
            to begin*.

NICKI   Whenever you're ready.

                              *

DAN   You know he's completely smitten.

SARAH   No he's not.

DAN   Oh come on.
            *Sarah, it's so amazing how you negotiated those
            difficult moral dilemmas*.

SARAH   He wasn't like that.

DAN   And in first aid last week, you could tell he was
            a fan of the mouth-to-mouth

SARAH   I think that's enough.

DAN   and obviously he finds the whole nurse–doctor
            thing a bit kinky.

SARAH   Dan.
            I know it's your thing to be funny, right?

DAN   –

SARAH   Right?

DAN   I guess.

SARAH   And Lisa laughed at all your jokes and it was great,
            yeah?

DAN   –

SARAH   Some advice: stop. You'll go further.

            A beat.

DAN   You should be careful, that's all.

SARAH   Careful.

DAN   Cos it's pretty obvious to everyone.
            And he likes you.
            And there's no one else, we're all about a decade
            older and I'm… I can be a very annoying person.

SARAH   –

DAN   He's just very clearly

SARAH   What? Vulnerable? Lonely? Forlorn? You don't
            need to patronise him.

DAN   I'm saying this is a job, that's all it is.

SARAH   Maybe to you.

            A beat.

DAN   Fine. I've said my piece. It's out there.

SARAH   Okay.

DAN   And ignore it, whatever, I don't care, I'd actually
            just like us to get on when we're out there.

SARAH   Yeah.
           Well.
           Obviously that'd be good.

                              *

           NICKI*'s phone goes off.*

NICKI   Bollocks. Sorry. I'm ignoring it, I'm ignoring it.

           She looks at her phone. Then silences it and puts it away.

           Dan, can you read it out.

           DAN *is holding an index card and a cup of coffee. Everyone else stands around him.*

           A vibrating sound is heard and NICKI *sighs. She looks at her phone. Then thinks for a moment.*

           Okay, I have to take this.

           NICKI *answers –*

           Hey, one sec.
           Stay in the room, read the thing out, I'll be two minutes.

           – and then leaves.

DAN   Tea break?

SARAH   We should get started.

DAN   C'mon, live a little.

KHALED   I'd like to hear it.

           DAN *does a dramatic sigh. Then he reads from the card.*

DAN   Ahem.
           'You are a Medical Provider dealing with
           a vulnerable Primary Actor, whom you have given
           a lot of your care and attention to. You are aware that
           this Primary Actor requires a lot of support but you
           are also aware that your mission will soon be coming

to a close. You are not sure how this Primary Actor
will react but you need to deliver the news clearly
whilst also understanding their vulnerability.'
So we need a Medical Provider.
And apparently we need someone to play a refugee.
Primary Actor.

Pause.

KHALED   I don't mind.

DAN   Yeah?

KHALED   Yeah.

DAN   You sure?

KHALED   Why, is that a problem?

DAN   No, I mean, I'm not trying to be
          like
          patronising or anything.

KHALED   Right.

DAN   Just after yesterday.

KHALED   I can handle a role-play.

DAN   Obviously.

KHALED   I can do a fucking role-play.

DAN   No. Yeah. Ignore me.

SARAH   I think he can decide for himself.

DAN   Absolutely.

          A beat.

SARAH   I'll be the Medical Provider.

DAN   Amazing.

          A beat. SARAH *and* KHALED *stand opposite
          each other now.*

          You'll fucking nail it dude.

                            *

SARAH   You need food.

KHALED   I'm alright.

SARAH   No, you're annoyed, you need food.

            SARAH *goes over to her bag, starts rooting around in it.*

            KHALED *watches on.*

KHALED   I'm not annoyed.

SARAH   –

KHALED   Okay I'm a bit annoyed.

            SARAH *still doesn't reply, she finds a falafel wrap in her bag.*

            It's just sometimes he fucks me off and it doesn't
            help having him
            There.
            All the time.

SARAH   I know.

KHALED   I don't need to be told what to do.

SARAH   So ignore him.

            SARAH *holds out the wrap.*

KHALED   What's that?

SARAH   I actually remembered a sandwich today. Take half.

KHALED   I've got lunch.

SARAH   But I hate being in debt.

KHALED   –

SARAH   M&S falafel wrap: if Tesco's gourmet then this
            is… Michelin Star or whatever, sorry I lost
            confidence in my own joke there.

KHALED   –

SARAH   What is it?

KHALED   I don't love falafel.

SARAH   Seriously?

KHALED   What, cos I'm Arab?

SARAH   No. That's not

KHALED   –

SARAH   No!

KHALED   I'm joking.

SARAH   Just take it please.

           KHALED does so.

           It's chickpeas, chickpeas won't kill you.

           *Then he sits up against the back wall and starts
           eating. SARAH looks at him.*

KHALED   It's quite good actually.

SARAH   I know.

           A beat. SARAH sits down next to KHALED.

           Consider it a peace offering.

KHALED   For what?

SARAH   For not knowing what to say. Yesterday. And then
           leaving you on your own.

KHALED   It's alright.

SARAH   No, it was shitty of me.

KHALED   I get in a mood, no one wants to deal with that.

SARAH   That's not true.

           The two eat. In silence. For a while.

           Did you, um, did you say it's only been five months?

KHALED   Uh-huh.

SARAH   That's not long.

KHALED   –

SARAH   You, um, you must miss him.

KHALED   We were thinking of going back around now but obviously…

SARAH   –

KHALED   Just to see family.

SARAH   Are they alright?

KHALED   I think so but…

KHALED doesn't finish the thought. They carry on eating…

SARAH   Are you alright?

KHALED   Uh-huh.

…until KHALED finishes the wrap. Brushes crumbs away. Looks at SARAH.

Thank you.

*

DAN   Mostly it's thinking about dying.

The whole group is sat around, listening to DAN.

Like in three weeks we'll be in this place that keeps appearing on my phone cos a hundred people are dead, two hundred, a thousand, whatever, the numbers are
Yeah.
Sometimes I'm scared I'm gonna die.
And sometimes I'm scared we won't be able to deal with it all.
And sometimes I'm scared the loos are gonna be shit.

*

SARAH and KHALED are alone.

SARAH   Wahad.

KHALED   Uh-huh.

SARAH   Tnain.

KHALED   Uh-huh.

SARAH   Talata.

KHALED   Talata.

SARAH   Talata.

KHALED   Talata.

SARAH   Which is what I said: Talata!
             Arba'a.

KHALED   Not really.

SARAH   Khaled.

KHALED   Keep going.

SARAH   Hamsa.
             Sitta.

KHALED   Come again?

SARAH   Sitta.

KHALED   Come again?

SARAH   Piss off I'm trying!

KHALED   With that accent?

SARAH   Sitta.
             Saba'a.
             Timaniya.
             Tisa'a. Tisa'a.
             Shit.
             Tisa'a.
             Stop laughing.

KHALED   I'm not.

SARAH   You fucking are – you do it!

KHALED   Mate I can count to ten.

SARAH   Alright.

KHALED   And you haven't even finished.

SARAH   Tisa'a.
Ashra.
Done.

Pause.

What?

KHALED   Nothing.

SARAH   What?

KHALED   That was quite good to be fair.

*

NICKI   Can we get some chairs gathered round?

No one moves.

Now please.

Chairs are dragged into the middle of the room. In the corner, DAN is staring at his phone.

Dan, if you could grab a seat.

DAN   Sure. Yeah.

They all sit.

NICKI   I don't know if anyone's seen the news.

No answer. DAN is still looking at his phone.

Hello?

DAN   I'm listening.

NICKI   Because apparently Lisa found out over the
weekend
from a colleague
that a story was coming out about, um…

DAN   The abuse.

SARAH   What?

NICKI   Okay. So you saw.

KHALED   Saw what?

NICKI   Look, I spent lunch on the phone with management and Lisa formally quit and handed in a complaint.

DAN   I told you she quit.

NICKI   At the start of the week.

SARAH   Sorry, what is her complaint?

NICKI   It's complicated.

DAN   That a bunch of people demanded sex in exchange for medicine.

NICKI   Yeah.   SARAH   Holy shit.
         Alright.
         Yeah.

DAN   That's what BBC's saying.

NICKI   It was only two of them. Actually.

KHALED   Only two what?

NICKI   It was two members of the organisation:
         a pharmacist and a logistics manager. Both men.

KHALED   How many refugees?

NICKI   It's still being figured out.

DAN   That means they don't know.

NICKI   Because we are in the process of uncovering evidence.
         Okay?
         And we can't solve everything at once.
         Despite what everyone seems to think.

SARAH   So what are you solving?

NICKI   It's not me, there's a whole
         There is an investigation, way above my pay.
         The two are suspended.
         There is an ongoing review and
         Um

	Sorry, I'm trying to remember what else they told me…
DAN	The article says there were like a dozen people doing it.
NICKI	Oh. Yeah. That's an unreliable witness.
SARAH	Are you serious?
NICKI	–
SARAH	I said are you serious?
NICKI	Yes. And I am angry. Okay? But I don't think it helps.
DAN	Did you know either of them?
NICKI	One of them.
DAN	One of them – what, you trained him?
NICKI	–
DAN	And he went to the same place we're going?

Pause.

NICKI	I want to ask if anyone has any thoughts or feelings. Because it's important to speak but it's also important we stay on track.
SARAH	Is that what they said to do?
NICKI	How would people feel about that?
SARAH	What, we just say some stuff and move on?
NICKI	–
SARAH	Did they only tell you cos of the news story?
NICKI	I'd like to hear everyone's thoughts.

Pause.

DAN   I'm okay with it.

SARAH   C'mon. Really?

DAN   Why, you want to stop everything?

SARAH   It's not great what just happened.

DAN   So you want to stop doing your job because someone else is acting like a dickhead?

SARAH   I'm still going despite the fact you're here.

NICKI   Sarah.

SARAH   Dan, a whole bunch of people just got caught abusing refugees.

DAN   Yes.

SARAH   IN OUR FUCKING CHARITY.

NICKI   Okay, this is

SARAH   You just said there could be a dozen of them.

NICKI   It is two.

SARAH   Oh so that's absolutely fine.

DAN   And they've been caught.
          Yeah?
          So shall we stop it with all the *Guardian* moral bollocks?

SARAH   Piss off.

DAN   If I want your opinion I can just go on Twitter.

KHALED   Dan, will you leave it.

          A beat.

          I'd like to know what happens next.

NICKI   What happens next.

KHALED   Yes.

NICKI   I mean there's the investigation.
          There's the results of that.

KHALED   With us.

NICKI   We'll um
I am around if people want to speak one-on-one.
I encourage it, it's important.
But otherwise we should keep going.

Pause.

SARAH   Well?

KHALED   Okay.

*

NICKI   Is there an explanation?

SARAH   –

NICKI   You don't want to give me an explanation?

SARAH   I… Yeah, I have permission.

NICKI   From who?

SARAH   Your government.

NICKI   Can I see?

SARAH   They said border guards would be informed, they said there wouldn't be a problem.

NICKI   All medicines brought into the country are charged a surplus customs tax. This tax costs one hundred British pounds, it can be paid in full to me.

SARAH   Well. Um. I wasn't told about this.

NICKI   It's new.

SARAH   Can I see… proof?

NICKI   Like what?

SARAH   Like a document. Like something that tells me that what you're doing is legal.

NICKI   I'm saying it is legal.

SARAH   Can you verify it?

NICKI	Are you calling me a liar?
SARAH	No. No. I simply want certainty.
NICKI	My word is certainty.
	SARAH *thinks*. NICKI *watches her.*
SARAH	What if I call my embassy?
NICKI	You don't have a phone.
SARAH	It's in my pocket.
NICKI	Show me.
SARAH	I mean. You told me to put my phone away so…
NICKI	So what?
SARAH	So I *would* have it, if we were actually here but
NICKI	But right now you do not.
SARAH	C'mon, this is
NICKI	Take control Sarah, have fun with it.
SARAH	I'm not paying you.
NICKI	Then I can't let you through.
SARAH	–
NICKI	Take out your purse.
SARAH	No.
NICKI	Are you causing trouble?
SARAH	No but if this was real then I could just call someone up and they would
NICKI	You speak Arabic?
SARAH	I'm speaking to you, aren't I?
NICKI	But you don't have a number to call. So take out your purse.
	SARAH *laughs – maybe it's more of a scoff.*
	One hundred or I will arrest you.

SARAH   This is ridiculous.

NICKI   Stay in it.

SARAH   I am in it.

NICKI   –

SARAH   This medicine is needed to stop people dying because right now there is a shortage and if your government would cooperate a bit more then we wouldn't have to carry bandages and antibiotics and sterilising fluid across a border.

NICKI   Your job is to stop people dying?

SARAH   Yes.

NICKI   Which people?

SARAH   In a refugee camp. In the north.

NICKI   You are a doctor?

SARAH   Yes.

NICKI   You help the refugees?

SARAH   Yes.

NICKI   We already have doctors.

SARAH   Not enough and not enough with the skills we provide.

NICKI   So you are better doctors?

SARAH   I don't know.

NICKI   And you believe they deserve better doctors? Better than people who are born here?

SARAH   No, that's

NICKI   I was born here.

SARAH   You have a job.

NICKI   Sometimes I am paid, sometimes not.

SARAH   Is this what the index card says?

NICKI   Don't give in to it.

SARAH   The people we help are put in a camp, they have
             nothing, there's no one else to help.

NICKI   I have a daughter in hospital, it costs money, you
             do not help her.

SARAH   And I'm sorry about that.

NICKI   So it's one hundred.

SARAH   You keep saying.

NICKI   And you do nothing.

SARAH   –

NICKI   Stand up to me.

SARAH   I… I refuse to give in to blackmail.

NICKI   Tell me again.

SARAH   I'll track down your manager you corrupt piece of
             shit and I'll tell him you're, you're

NICKI   Blackmailing a rich westerner at customs, oh no,
             he'll be absolutely furious!

SARAH   –

NICKI   Tactics. Tactics.

             Then SARAH *goes over to her bag, takes out her
             purse.*

SARAH   One hundred, yes? Do you take card?

NICKI   I'm sorry?

SARAH   Cos I don't have any cash. Card?

             For a moment, NICKI *watches* SARAH. *Then*
             NICKI *notices* SARAH's *necklace and points to it.*

NICKI   What's that?

SARAH   Oh. No, this is, um, from a boyfriend.

NICKI   Worth a lot?

SARAH   A small amount.

           NICKI *holds out her hand.*

           No, I'm not handing it over.

NICKI   Then you don't get through.

SARAH   Okay. Sure. So I've failed this fucking little
           blackmail fucking role-play thing have I?

NICKI   It's not about failing.

SARAH   But have I?

           NICKI *gestures, as if to say 'hand it over'.*

           No.

           NICKI *gestures again.*

           No: the necklace is of great sentimental value but
           of little to no financial value.
           It will not help. I cannot help. And if you keep
           asking for
           money, anything
           Number one: I will scream.
           Number two: my organisation will come down on
           you like a tonne of bricks.
           Is that what you want?

NICKI   Yes.

                              *

           SARAH *packs her bag.* KHALED *flicks through
           his phone.*

SARAH   Are you getting the bus?

KHALED   Mm-hm.

SARAH   Always shit round here, aren't they?

           KHALED *doesn't reply and* SARAH *hovers for
           a moment.*

           Staring at the internet's not going to help, you know.

KHALED   I know.

SARAH   Everyone's got an opinion.

           Pause. KHALED *looks up*.

KHALED   So, what, your opinion is you're gonna quit?

SARAH   I'm sorry?

KHALED   I dunno, you seemed a bit

SARAH   A bit what?

KHALED   Like not exactly happy.

SARAH   Not exactly, no.

KHALED   –

SARAH   I mean, I'm still figuring it out but it looks bad.

KHALED   Right.

SARAH   And I don't know if they're actually doing
           anything.

KHALED   Right.

SARAH   So… I mean it's not like you got pissed off.

KHALED   I'm angry.

SARAH   You don't sound it.

KHALED   What you don't believe me?

SARAH   –

KHALED   Look, I get how people think. And I get that we're
           A bunch of white people turn up in a refugee camp,
           try to save the world, fuck it up instead – that
           makes me angry.

SARAH   You're not
           white.

KHALED   Oh am I not?

SARAH   –

KHALED   But I've got skills, I can save lives, I can do good, right?

SARAH   Yes.

KHALED   So I'm not quitting because other people think it's all a game.

SARAH   A game?

KHALED   Not a game but

SARAH   But what?

KHALED   Nothing.

SARAH   No, tell me.

KHALED   Lisa quit because she cares more about her morals than dying brown people.

           A beat.

SARAH   Is that what you'd think if I left?

KHALED   No.

SARAH   Fuck you, that's exactly what you'd think.

KHALED   No.

SARAH   It was two men, in management positions, targeting women and you don't think that's a problem?

KHALED   I know it's a problem.

SARAH   But not enough of a problem?

KHALED   Not when people get pissed off about fucking optics and it's so clearly any excuse not to actually do something.

SARAH   Sorry, it's just optics now?

KHALED   –

SARAH   Oh my god, can you actually not answer?

KHALED   I think there's very good reasons for you to leave. But it is also true that you have a choice and I don't feel like I have a choice.

SARAH   You're making it sound simpler than it is.

KHALED   –

SARAH   Okay. I don't need this.

KHALED   I'm just saying what I see.

           Pause.

SARAH   I was coming in here to ask if you wanted to grab
           a drink.
           That's what this was.
           I had it planned: saying I'm free – tonight – not
           running off like the other day.

KHALED   That would be nice.

SARAH   Yeah, well, if you're gonna be a dickhead what's
           the point?

KHALED   Sarah.

           Then SARAH *heads over to the door.*

SARAH   No, he can't even text a girl, what did I think was
           gonna happen?

KHALED   I would really like to, to

SARAH   To what?

           SARAH *hovers.* KHALED *doesn't answer.*
           SARAH *keeps walking over to the door –*

KHALED   I've got this memory of him.

           – and then she stops.

           That I keep… And I keep wanting to… He's sat in
           his armchair and he's got worry beads in one hand,
           flicking through them
           clicking and clicking
           and he's got the remote in the other and it's Al
           Jazeera on the TV – on mute – so he can read the
           headlines and listen to a CD of this old jazz band
           from Beirut in the seventies.

SARAH   –

KHALED   And the CD's still in the player – I can't take it out,
          I can't listen to it either.

SARAH   –

KHALED   Sorry.

SARAH   Don't be sorry.

KHALED   It's fucking weird and horrible doing all this.

SARAH   You don't have to.

          A long pause.

          Would you like a bit of space?

KHALED   When you said you were free tonight.

SARAH   –

KHALED   I'm trying to figure out what you meant.
          Like, is it just a couple of mates grabbing a drink
          or…

SARAH   Or what?

KHALED   Or something a bit more…

SARAH   Wow. Okay.

KHALED   Okay?

SARAH   –

KHALED   What?

SARAH   What? Am I not even worth a chat-up line?

          A beat. KHALED *laughs.*

KHALED   I mean, I could agree with you. That the buses
          round here are complete dogshit.

SARAH   That's not a chat-up line.

KHALED   I could say let's Uber it somewhere but too many
          chuggers got me this month and now my account's
          empty.

          Now SARAH *laughs.*

SARAH   Where would we get an Uber to?

KHALED   Anywhere you want. And on the way, maybe I'd
          say something about your eyes.

SARAH   My eyes.

KHALED   Or your lips.

          Pause.

SARAH   You know what I was gonna say? Cos I actually
          had a good chat-up line.

KHALED   Oh yeah?

SARAH   Cos you told me you don't like people screwing
          you around.

KHALED   –

SARAH   But I was gonna say that
          I do.
          Sometimes.

          The two look at each other.

                              *

          Someone is asleep in the room.

          A phone alarm goes off and we see NICKI *waking
          up, stretching, putting on her watch, checking her
          phone. She takes out wet wipes and mops under her
          armpits, she sprays some deodorant as well as
          a load of perfume. She trawls through her bag and
          pulls out a spare T-shirt. She smells it – not exactly
          fresh – then puts it on anyway.*

          As she does, DAN *enters.*

DAN   Shit.

NICKI   Jesus, Dan.

DAN   Sorry, should I

NICKI   Do you mind?

DAN   Yeah. No. I was just

Except DAN *doesn't move.*

I just wanted a chat before the others arrive.

NICKI   Can you give me five minutes?

DAN   –

NICKI   Dan.

DAN   Are you sleeping here?

NICKI   We're not discussing me.

DAN   –

NICKI   Hello?

DAN   Why are you sleeping here?

A beat.

NICKI   Look, if this is about Lisa, frankly I think she left for the wrong reasons.

DAN   No, I get that.

NICKI   I think it was about wanting to keep her nose clean.

DAN   I'm not interested in Lisa.
I was, um, interested in
Like management stuff.

NICKI   And you want to talk about it now?

DAN   I'm just thinking about what happens after this.

NICKI   I don't decide what happens after this.

DAN   But you have a say.
A conversation happens.

NICKI   Yeah.

DAN   So. I dunno. Look, I swear I'm not going to say anything about, um

NICKI   –

DAN   I would appreciate a chat, that's it.

NICKI   Okay.

DAN   And if you ever need to talk or…

NICKI   Thank you.

DAN   –

NICKI   So can you

DAN   Yeah.
          Right.
          I'll, um

          Pause.

          When I was looking after Mum, I'd spend nights
          away. Like in hospital accommodation. If I couldn't
          Like if I couldn't handle it.

NICKI   –

DAN   I just thought I should say.

NICKI   I didn't know you looked after her.

DAN   Almost a year now, yeah.

NICKI   Is she

DAN   Old – and needs help – but she's fine – it's just
          some people were such shitbags, other doctors, you
          know, they could be…
          Like the point is, no one really got it.

NICKI   Right.

DAN   Anyway. Whatever. I'm gonna

          And DAN *is about to leave when –*

NICKI   My sister has MS.
          Early stages but it's not going away so

DAN   I'm sorry.

NICKI   I live with her and look after her and spend half the
          day on the phone to her.
          The flat we've got is so
          tiny and

	stuffy and This is temporary.
DAN	That's really good what you're doing.
NICKI	She's my sister.
DAN	But it's tough. It's really tough.

Pause.

NICKI	If you need time for your mum.
DAN	She'd kill me.
NICKI	–
DAN	I promised her I'd speak to you, that's all.
NICKI	We'll find a moment.
DAN	I don't want it out of pity.
NICKI	I know.

A beat.

C'mon. If I stay in this room any longer I'll suffocate.

*

SARAH *is sat,* KHALED *is stood – a little out of breath – still holding his bag.*

KHALED	The buses were a mess, I thought I'd be so late.
SARAH	–
KHALED	You okay?
SARAH	Fine. You?
KHALED	Yeah. Like I had a really good time yesterday so
SARAH	Yeah?
KHALED	Yeah, it was really

A beat.

And I'm sorry, if you…

SARAH   What?

KHALED   –

SARAH   Oh I don't care.

KHALED   It just kinda seems like you might care.

SARAH   I don't.

KHALED   Okay.

           Pause.

SARAH   I mean I wasn't sure what it meant but I didn't care.

KHALED   It's not that I didn't want to.

SARAH   Okay.

KHALED   It's just that I
           Like when do people ever just do that?
           Like just cuddling or whatever, I kinda think
           I needed it.

SARAH   –

KHALED   And you know I slept like a log.
           So whatever you think was going on, it wasn't
           really going on cos I
           Honestly, straight through.
           And normally I get some messed-up dreams but
           last night...
           Sorry, I'm exhausted so I had a coffee and a Red
           Bull and now I'm

SARAH   It's alright.

KHALED   I'm all over the place and I really need a wee but
           I didn't want you to think
           anything bad.
           Cos it wasn't.

SARAH   Good.

           And KHALED *is about to speak when* DAN *walks
           in holding a coffee cup.*

DAN   Oh hello. The two lovebirds.

*

KHALED   Um. Hi. Come on in.

DAN   –

KHALED   So, yeah, I've got great news for you.

          A beat. DAN *and* KHALED *are opposite each
          other.* NICKI *and* SARAH *watch.*

          Cos, um, obviously you came in here, with a bullet
          wound.
          And, yeah, it's healing really well actually, no
          problems with the infection, so
          We're planning to discharge you back into the
          camp.
          So. Yes. You're welcome to leave whenever is
          convenient for you but ideally soon.

DAN   I can't.

KHALED   Okay. Um. Why is that?

DAN   It's painful.

KHALED   Well. No. We believe you're now all good to go.

DAN   But it still hurts.

KHALED   And obviously the wound can be sore but that
          doesn't mean you're not well enough to, um, to

DAN   I can't go back.

KHALED   Ali, it's alright.

DAN   I'm scared.

KHALED   –

DAN   I'm scared, please don't make me.

KHALED   I thought you were in pain?

DAN   I don't know I just know that there are men in the
          camp and they threaten me and I'm safe here and
          I am not safe in there.

KHALED   –

DAN   Keep me in the hospital another night.

KHALED   We, um, have other patients to look after.

DAN   They could kill me if you send me back.

KHALED   Okay, no, this is

DAN   I am not safe.

KHALED   I thought your wound hadn't healed, that's the role-play.

DAN   I'm just trying to get some help, I don't know anything about a role-play.

KHALED   No, the role-play is that he thinks his wound hasn't healed and I'm trying to tell him that it has.

NICKI   –

SARAH   –

KHALED   You have to go back into the camp, Ali, we no longer need to monitor you.

DAN   If I go back they'll kill me.

KHALED   Who will?

DAN   The men who know that I'm gay.

KHALED   What?

DAN   Yes.

KHALED   You can't just

DAN   What?

         A beat.

KHALED   He wouldn't say that.

DAN   Why not?

KHALED   Cos he's... he's Arab, Arabs aren't

DAN   What, Arabs aren't gay?

KHALED   You know what I mean.

DAN   I don't.

KHALED   People aren't open about it like that.

DAN   And you know them all do you?

KHALED   I know he wouldn't tell me, I'm a foreigner.

DAN   But I just have.

KHALED   But you can't just make it up.

DAN   I haven't.

KHALED   –

DAN   Hello? I thought you want to do well on these things.

NICKI   Can we keep it on track.

KHALED   Yeah, just give me…

Pause.

Um, so obviously we're a hospital and we can't provide the sort of
The protection that you're after and we're happy to link you to another, um

DAN   Sorry, can I speak to a doctor?

KHALED   I've been sent here by a doctor.

DAN   No offence but I don't want to speak to a nurse about this, I'd like to speak to the doctor who's been looking after me.

KHALED   –

DAN   And you can tell him everything I've told you or I'll tell him I just need to speak to someone who has the power to let me stay.
Please.

KHALED   Dan.

DAN   Ali.

KHALED   This isn't

           Pause.

           Fuck. Okay. Can we discuss it already?

                              *

SARAH   This is kinda stupid but I got you a present.

           Just SARAH *and* KHALED *in the room.*

           SARAH *takes some worry beads out of her bag.*

           If you want.
           Cos I found them over the weekend – *Misbahah* –
           is that how you say it?

KHALED   Yeah.

SARAH   And I thought of you.
           Like, what you said about your dad. Cos you
           couldn't find his, right?

           SARAH *holds them out and* KHALED *takes them.*

KHALED   Right.

SARAH   And I know how good they are for clearing your
           head or whatever.
           I mean, they're more for prayer but still.

KHALED   They're beautiful.

SARAH   Aren't they?

KHALED   –

SARAH   Are they like his?

           KHALED *doesn't reply, he just looks at the beads.*

                              *

NICKI   When do we say no?
           I'm curious about that because we listen.
           And we hand over agency and power, that's
           our work.
           But what if the… if the world view of the people
           we're giving that power to is…

Pause. The group is sat in a circle, listening.

We had an incident a few years back, separate
mission, we were coordinating care with the elders
of a village.
Medical facility.
Emergency care.
They were on the outskirts of a civil war so...
And they ask us if we can perform FGM.
There's a group of young girls, prepubescent,
waiting.
And that's clear, we don't recognise it as a medical
procedure, we say no.
But then the village organises it.
They find a local doctor – I don't know if you
could call him a doctor – but he specifically doesn't
do it on our premises.
The point is we're not political.
We try not to be.
But also we have a duty of care,
And if we want to be rigorous then we need to
examine our decisions so what do we do?

KHALED   Were you there?

NICKI   I'm asking what you would do.

KHALED   But what did they do?

NICKI   It's theoretical.

DAN   As in it didn't happen?

NICKI   As in it happened but I'm saying – for us, now –
            it's theoretical.

*

SARAH   Hey.

KHALED   Hi.

SARAH   Are you alright?

KHALED   No one else is here?

SARAH   Just me.

KHALED   Do you mind?

SARAH   No.

           A beat. SARAH *and* KHALED *are alone.*

KHALED   Sorry. Just figuring out, um

SARAH   Is there someone you want to see?

KHALED   Oh. Yes. I am meant to have an appointment.

SARAH   With who? Cos I can take a look. If you want.

KHALED   Okay.

SARAH   –

KHALED   I have a
           a wound
           it got infected
           but is fine
           but they say to have a check-up.

SARAH   Okay.

KHALED   Should I…

SARAH   Sure. I mean, if we're doing it properly.

           SARAH *smiles.*

           KHALED *hesitates – then takes off his top. There
           is a bandage on his arm and* SARAH *examines it.*

           Then she removes the bandage to reveal a cut.

           From a bullet?

KHALED   Yes.

SARAH   Does it still hurt?

KHALED   Yes.

SARAH   But it looks like it's improving.

KHALED   –

SARAH   This is going to sting a little.

> SARAH *disinfects the cut*. KHALED *winces*.
> SARAH *starts to put on a clean bandage*.

How's that?

KHALED   Good.

SARAH   My hands aren't too cold?

KHALED   They're warm.

SARAH   I'll just be a moment.

KHALED   Thank you.

SARAH   No need to thank me, um

KHALED   Ali. My name is Ali.

SARAH   Okay. Hi Ali.

KHALED   Do you have a name?

SARAH   Um. Laura.

KHALED   Laura.
I like that name.
Thank you Laura.

> SARAH *finishes putting on the bandage, steps
> back. Pause*.

In the camp, very little people are like this.

SARAH   Is that right?

KHALED   Lots of mean people, angry people.

SARAH   I'm sure that's not true.

KHALED   Bullies.

SARAH   You must have some friends.

KHALED   My father was shot on the border, he died in my
arms, I know no one else.

> *Pause*.

SARAH   You must miss him.

KHALED   A lot, yes.

SARAH   I can imagine.

KHALED   Can you?

                    Pause.

SARAH   I, um, I lost my father too. When I was very young.
                    It stays with you.

KHALED   –

SARAH   And I have dreams too, you know.

KHALED   Dreams?

SARAH   Every now and then.

KHALED   When I dream, it is only about him.
                    Can I say this?

SARAH   Of course.

KHALED   I see him and he is in my arms and he is bleeding
                    and he is squeezing my hand and shouting and
                    shouting but I do not understand a word, I am so
                    scared. Every night.

SARAH   –

KHALED   You do not want to hear this.

SARAH   I do.

KHALED   I am speaking to a beautiful girl and I am talking
                    rubbish.

SARAH   It's not rubbish.

KHALED   –

SARAH   And beautiful is a bit...

KHALED   –

SARAH   Maybe you should put your, um, your T-shirt

KHALED   Oh.

SARAH   If you want.

KHALED   And if I do not?

           A beat. SARAH *laughs. And* KHALED *winks at* SARAH.

SARAH   Did you just wink at me?

KHALED   I am putting on my T-shirt.

SARAH   I saw you.

KHALED   I cannot remember.

SARAH   You can't remember.

KHALED   Maybe.

SARAH   Maybe.

KHALED   –

SARAH   I'm trying to be a professional here: is there anything else I can do for you Ali?

KHALED   –

SARAH   No?

KHALED   I am supposed to be looking for work.

SARAH   Work. Okay.

KHALED   Will you help me find some?

           A beat.

SARAH   Well I know that if we have a medical facility going up then we try to partner with an organisation.

KHALED   Okay.

SARAH   But I'm also very conscious of getting your hopes up.

KHALED   Anything is good.

SARAH   I know but

KHALED   And I have skills.

SARAH   Skills. Like what?

KHALED   I was at university. Back home.

SARAH   You have a degree?

KHALED   My university shut. The men with guns.

SARAH   I see.

KHALED   Does this mean there is nothing?

SARAH   No, not at all.

KHALED   So you will find me something?

SARAH   I'm saying it doesn't mean we can't try. Okay?

KHALED   You promise?

SARAH   I'm not supposed to make promises.

KHALED   But for me.
           Just a small promise.

           A beat.

SARAH   It might take a while.

KHALED   But I am not leaving.

                            *

NICKI   Sarah?

SARAH   Yes. Sorry. I don't understand why you're asking me.

NICKI   It's a check-in, that's all.

SARAH   Except you're asking me instead of speaking
           to him.

NICKI   I thought you might have an insight.

SARAH   An insight.

NICKI   Because you seem to get on well.

SARAH   –

NICKI   Look, if something's private then it's private, it's
           not for me to say…

SARAH   Yes.

NICKI   I'm just trying to make sure that Khaled feels
         settled.

SARAH   *Kh*-aled

NICKI   Excuse me?

SARAH   You've spent the whole time pronouncing it with
         a hard *K* but it's *Kh*-a-led.
         Back of the throat.

NICKI   Right.

SARAH   And he's fine.

NICKI   Thank you Sarah.

SARAH   Sorry.

NICKI   No. Thank you for pointing it out. It's been noted.

*

The group is sat around.

SARAH   I found the accent distracting.

DAN   Why?

SARAH   Cos I couldn't concentrate when you're putting on
         an accent.

DAN   It worked for me.

NICKI   How about we focus on how the situation was
         managed?

         A beat.

KHALED   I thought Sarah handled it well.

DAN   Surprising.

NICKI   Let him finish.

KHALED   As in, because Dan pushed her to reveal what had
         happened and then asked her to correct things in
         a way that was really, um, forceful.

DAN   Charles.

KHALED   What?

DAN   You're saying I did it but it was a role-play.

NICKI   It was you in a role-play.

DAN   It was Charles and I wasn't being, *um, forceful*.

KHALED   Well I just thought Sarah was really calm and
           effective.

           A beat.

NICKI   How about the way Dan broached the subject
           matter?

SARAH   I actually found Dan's demeanour a little
           aggressive.

DAN   Charles's demeanour.

SARAH   Sure.

DAN   I mean, you were pretty defensive.

SARAH   I was not.

DAN   Also, I'm accusing you of having an inappropriate
           relationship with a refugee, I'm probably going to
           get aggressive, yeah.

SARAH   Okay.

DAN   Oh come on.

SARAH   I said okay.

           A beat.

DAN   I was the right amount of aggressive.

NICKI   Let's just do it again. Without the accent.

                              *

           KHALED *sits with his back against the wall.*
           SARAH *is lying down, with her head resting on
           her bag. She's looking at her phone while he
           presses his thumbs on either side of her head.*

KHALED   Who are you messaging?

SARAH   Just a mate. Yeah just there.

            KHALED *squeezes a little more.*

KHALED   Yeah?

SARAH   That's it, that's good. God, this headache just
            came on.

KHALED   Or it's Dan.

SARAH   Yeah, I've got a headache called Dan.

            SARAH *finishes sending a message, puts her
            phone down.*

KHALED   What?

SARAH   Nothing.

            Silence.

            Do you only ever go out with white girls?

            KHALED *doesn't reply.* SARAH *sits up.*

            Too much?

KHALED   Is that what this is, we're going out?

SARAH   Don't ignore the question.

KHALED   –

SARAH   –

KHALED   I've gone out with lots of girls.

SARAH   Lots of girls, hey, that sounds fun.

KHALED   You know what I mean.

SARAH   What, like more than a handful?

KHALED   –

SARAH   I don't care, you shouldn't be embarrassed.

KHALED   I'm not.

SARAH   So?

KHALED   So… Yeah, maybe.

SARAH   Maybe what?

KHALED   Maybe if you had to look for a pattern
            of types of
            women
            which I'm not doing but if you're asking and if
            I have to say

SARAH   then it's all white women.

KHALED   Potentially.

SARAH   Potentially.

KHALED   What about you?

SARAH   No white women, no.

KHALED   C'mon.

SARAH   What?

KHALED   –

SARAH   The last one was called Tom; you're called Khaled.

KHALED   Are they always young?

SARAH   He's thirty-five.

            Pause.

KHALED   So what are we doing tonight?

SARAH   You know, I liked it when you called me beautiful.
            Earlier.

KHALED   Yeah?

SARAH   Yeah.

KHALED   I mean cos it's true.

            Another pause. SARAH*'s phone goes off and she
            checks it.*

            Sarah?

SARAH   Sorry.

KHALED   –

SARAH   I've got plans tonight.

KHALED   Okay.

SARAH   Don't give me that, I can't cancel now.

KHALED   No, I get it.

SARAH   We said another time.

> SARAH *kisses* KHALED *on the cheek. Then she stands, starts packing her bag.* KHALED *hovers.*

> What is it, what are you thinking?

KHALED   Honestly, the thought of sitting at home, opposite Mum, eating dinner in silence, stuck in my head all night.

SARAH   I know.

KHALED   So cancel.

SARAH   I can't.

KHALED   You can.

> SARAH *pauses, sighs.*

> Who are you meeting?

SARAH   Please don't.

KHALED   Is that who you're texting?

SARAH   I'm not answering that.

KHALED   I just wanna know who's more important than me.

SARAH   This isn't helpful.

KHALED   It is for me.

SARAH   No it's not.

KHALED   Are you sure? Cos, no offence, I don't think you really know what it's like to properly lose someone.

SARAH   You don't think I know?

KHALED   –

SARAH   Are you stupid?

KHALED   What, am I wrong?

SARAH   Yes.

A beat.

KHALED   Your dad?

SARAH *sort of shrugs.*

SARAH   I was young.

KHALED   I thought that was… Like why didn't you

SARAH   Cos we're not talking about it.

KHALED   –

SARAH   But I get it. And I get that it takes a long time.

Then SARAH *walks over to* KHALED, *kisses him on the lips.*

I will call you tonight and I will see you tomorrow, alright?

Then she walks out.

*

KHALED *is in the room. He's on his own, sitting against the back wall, staring at his phone.*

We hear a sound: a sort of electronic jingle coming from KHALED's *phone and we realise that he's on Duolingo, practising his Arabic. He says a couple of words in Arabic: not too advanced but not too basic and his accent is pretty convincing. He keeps going for a while.*

Then DAN *enters.* KHALED *quickly puts his phone away and looks at* DAN.

DAN   Hello.

KHALED   Hi.

DAN   You're here early.

KHALED   Am I?

DAN   Meeting Sarah or something?

        KHALED *doesn't reply.* DAN *dumps his bag in the corner.*

        How are things with her?

KHALED   What things?

DAN   He's going red.

KHALED   No.

DAN   Yes he is, he's going red.

KHALED   No.

DAN   Dude, I'm messing with you.

KHALED   You know what, we're doing really well.

DAN   Well that's great.

KHALED   So if you could just

DAN   Hey, no, I think she's nice.
        I mean, she's got too many opinions but
        she's nice.

        Pause.

        Do you, uh, do you communicate well with her?

KHALED   What?

DAN   I dunno
        I… I had an ex who was way older and he made it
        really intense really fucking quick, that's all.

KHALED   Okay.

DAN   I'm just trying to
        you know
        if she's in a good place.

KHALED   She's a big girl.

DAN   Okay. Well. I need coffee before we start, do you
            want one?

KHALED   I'm good.

DAN   Shout if you need anything.

            DAN *walks over to the door. Then he pauses.*

            I'm serious by the way. Like not just a coffee,
            anything, whatever, I'm here.

            KHALED *doesn't quite know how to respond.*

            As in, if you ever need
            man chat.

KHALED   Man chat?

DAN   Like someone who can go
            you know
            snap out of it.

KHALED   I'm sorry?

DAN   Just sometimes people need a kick up the arse. And
            I'm around.

KHALED   Okay.

DAN   What?

KHALED   A kick up the arse?

DAN   Or whatever. What's the look?

KHALED   No look.

DAN   Dude.

KHALED   Honestly?

DAN   Yeah I can handle a bit of honesty.

KHALED   I'm trying to figure out how seriously you take all
            this.

DAN   Is that a joke?

KHALED   I dunno, you're the funny man.

DAN   Oh that's good.

KHALED   Cos it's important what we're doing.

DAN   And I'm aware of that.

KHALED   –

DAN   I want this to be my career.

KHALED   Maybe that's the problem.

DAN   No, it means I put everything into it because it's my life, it is not a holiday.

KHALED   I never said it's a holiday.

DAN   Oh, I'm sorry, I mean it's not speed-dating. Not training to be a toy boy.

KHALED   Wow.

DAN   If we're talking about taking this thing seriously.

KHALED   And I'm talking about being here with the right people.

DAN   The right people?

KHALED   Uh-huh.

DAN   So you've got a superiority complex or something, is that it?

KHALED   No.

DAN   Like it's up to you to decide who's good enough?

KHALED   No.

DAN   And I'm not good enough? Cos I thought I was doing alright but clearly not.

KHALED   –

DAN   And Sarah, yeah, she's definitely good enough, is that right? And where did Lisa sit – if we're ranking people – or is she too much of a quitter? And then there's Nicki, she's not even medically qualified, I bet she's nowhere near fucking good enough.

           KHALED *doesn't have a reply.*

*

NICKI   'The border is closed. It has been closed because
             the government refuses to take in any more
             Primary Actors. This has caused a bottleneck,
             meaning many have been stranded in the no man's
             land between this country and their home country,
             without access to medical care. You are a Project
             Coordinator...'

             *The group is gathered round. NICKI is reading
             from an index card. She looks up for a moment.*

SARAH   I can do it.

NICKI   '...a Project Coordinator who has called on the
             government to open the border. You must speak to
             a representative from the Ministry of Health to
             ensure this happens.'

             A beat.

             I'm going to take this one actually. Because I've
             decided, um

             A beat.

             Sorry, I've done this the wrong way round.
             I was asked to go out because obviously we're
             struggling with numbers at the moment so
             I'll be on admin in a camp further south.
             It's been a while so.

DAN   What about your sister?

             Pause.

SARAH   What sister?

DAN   Shit, I didn't mean to
             That was a, ignore that, I didn't say that.

SARAH   What's going on?

NICKI   Shall we start the exercise?

DAN   I'm really sorry.

NICKI   Sarah?

DAN   I was just trying to

NICKI   I know.

DAN   I was trying to be a nice person.

NICKI   None of this is about being a nice person.
           None of this is about being a nice person.

           A beat.

           Sarah?

           SARAH *and* NICKI *stand opposite each other.*

                              *

SARAH   I got home and I couldn't really…

KHALED   Me neither.

SARAH   I ended up going down a rabbit hole reading
           articles about the *zakat*.

           SARAH *and* KHALED *are alone. A beat.*

           I mean obviously I knew about it before but I didn't
           know about it know about it.

KHALED   Okay.

           A beat.

SARAH   I guess I'm saying it was a shit night and would've
           been better with you there.
           And I missed you.

KHALED   Me too.

SARAH   And I tried calling.

KHALED   We were up late.

SARAH   Did you manage a good heart-to-heart?

KHALED   Not really.

SARAH   Did you try?

           KHALED *shrugs. Pause.*

           If no one was listening, what would you say?

KHALED   What do you mean?

SARAH   Like, your mum's in front of you and you can just
            shout anything in her face
            what would it be?

KHALED   –

SARAH   It's not a trick, I'm just trying to think of
            She's your mum, you should be able to speak to
            your mum.

KHALED   I know.

            A beat.

SARAH   You're not very good at all this are you?

                              *

            DAN*'s phone pings.*

DAN   That's me.

            He goes over to his bag. It pings again.

            Okay, yeah, two seconds.

            DAN *gets his phone out, checks it. The rest of the
            group waits.*

NICKI   We're in the middle of something.

DAN   I know, just give me…

            Except DAN *starts typing out a message –*

NICKI   Dan.

            – and keeps on typing.

            Then SARAH *walks over and tries to look at*
            DAN*'s phone.* DAN *hides it from her.*

DAN   What are you doing?

SARAH   What are you doing?

DAN   Nothing.

SARAH   Who's texting you?

DAN	Why do you care?
SARAH	Why are you being weird?
DAN	I'm not.
SARAH	Have you got a hot date?
DAN	No.
SARAH	Is someone sending naked pics?
DAN	No.
NICKI	Sarah.
SARAH	Are you sure about that? Let me see.
DAN	Piss off.
NICKI	Can we get started please?
SARAH	Yeah, can we get started please?
NICKI	Sarah.

Except DAN *keeps typing.*

SARAH	He's still typing!
NICKI	Dan.
DAN	–
SARAH	DAN. Who are you texting?
DAN	No one.
SARAH	DAN!
DAN	It's Lisa. Dipshit.

Pause.

SARAH	Why is she texting?
DAN	Does it matter?
NICKI	If it's about the investigation.
DAN	It's not.
SARAH	So what is it?
DAN	She's asking why I haven't quit.

KHALED   And?

DAN   And nothing.

SARAH   So why are you replying?

DAN   Cos she's saying they knew about the relationships
           for quite a while.

NICKI   That's not true.

SARAH   Relationships?

DAN   Whatever you call it.

SARAH   Abuse.

DAN   The point is she thinks they let it slide.

KHALED   I read one of them was a proper thing.

SARAH   Oh come on.

KHALED   He just happened to be giving her medicine.

SARAH   And then expecting sex?

DAN   Or she gave him sex and demanded medicine.

NICKI   Okay, I am done with our shit being in this room.
           Is that clear?
           We need to start.

                              *

           SARAH *and* KHALED *are alone. Each waits for
           the other to speak.*

SARAH   So...

KHALED   Yeah.

SARAH   If it's too weird.

KHALED   No.

SARAH   Cos we can stop.

           Pause.

           How does it feel?

KHALED   Fine.

SARAH   I mean actually.

KHALED   –

SARAH   Or, like, how do you feel?

KHALED   –

SARAH   How would Ali feel?
If he could say anything.
To anyone.
He might feel…

KHALED   Comforted.

SARAH   Comforted?

KHALED   Safe.
Here.
With you.

SARAH   That's good.

KHALED   Looked after, um

They're a bit closer to each other now.

maybe, turned on.

SARAH   Okay.

KHALED   What?

SARAH   No. Whatever Ali feels.

KHALED *looks around to make sure the coast
is clear.*

KHALED   I, um, I liked it when you gave me a check-up.

SARAH   Ali wants a check-up from the beautiful woman?

Now KHALED *laughs.*

You can't laugh, this is very serious.

KHALED   Sorry. Laura.

SARAH   Miss Laura.

KHALED   Miss Laura.

SARAH   Miss Laura wants to know what she can do to make
          it better.

KHALED   What she can *do*?

SARAH   Because we're alone.
          And she can do anything.

          KHALED *bites his lip. Now they're very close.*

          Tell me what you're thinking.
          In that head of yours.
          Whatever you want to let out.
          Even the dirtiest... little... secret.

KHALED   When Dad was dying he only spoke Arabic.

SARAH   What?

KHALED   Sorry, I don't know where that came from.

SARAH   It's okay.

KHALED   –

SARAH   Khaled?

KHALED   He spent two days lying in a hospital bed and he
          forgot all his English.

SARAH   Oh my god.

KHALED   He was so scared. And I didn't understand a word.

                              *

          NICKI *is sending a message on her phone.* DAN *is
          also there. He hovers nearby. Then takes a step
          forward, about to start a conversation.*

NICKI   It's alright.

DAN   –

NICKI   Please don't apologise.

DAN   Okay.

          She puts her phone away, looks at him.

NICKI   Actually, Dan, can we...

DAN   Yeah?

NICKI   When you said your mum pushed you to come here.

DAN   Uh-huh.

NICKI   Did she find it difficult?

DAN   Of course.

NICKI   Did you?

DAN   Not after I'd made the decision.

           Pause.

NICKI   I started looking for a carer, last night, just to
           pre-empt…

DAN   That's great.

NICKI   –

DAN   She'll be alright, you know, she'll get it.

           Pause.

NICKI   When I was twelve she kicked a kid in the balls cos
           he tried to kiss me and I didn't like it.
           I think he had to go to hospital.

           A beat. DAN *laughs.*

           I miss that.

DAN   She sounds bad-ass.

NICKI   She was.

                              *

           The group is sat in a semicircle, everyone watching
           KHALED.

KHALED   I'm not Muslim. I don't think.
           But I guess I grew up with… Dad would take me
           to mosque.
           And I guess I've thought about that a lot more.
           Recently.
           And one of the five pillars is that you give to charity.

It's called the *zakat*: it's a tax.
It means a moral purifier.
And it can be a legal thing as well – in some
countries – where my family's from they chop off
your hand if you don't do it.

–

That's a joke – is this what you meant?

NICKI   Keep going.

KHALED   Yeah.
I guess the bit that matters is you give a part of
your wealth to people who need it and it's never
even a question.
Everyone's involved and everyone just does it and
gets on with it and there's no, I dunno, there's none
of the bullshit and the… the…

–

Sorry.

*

SARAH   Has Lisa tried you as well?

KHALED   Mm-hm.

SARAH   And?

KHALED   I ignored it.

          A beat. It's just KHALED *and* SARAH.

          She messaged me ten minutes after Mum tried
          getting me to quit.

SARAH   What?

KHALED   –

SARAH   She tried to get you to quit?

          KHALED *shrugs.*

KHALED   She got angry. And then I got angry at her and told
          her it's my choice.

SARAH   I'm sorry, that sounds…

KHALED   –

SARAH   And it is your choice.

          KHALED *shrugs*.

          Khaled.

KHALED   I dunno.

SARAH   What else did she say?

KHALED   That I can't sort everything out by disappearing.
          That I should be with family.

SARAH   You should be wherever you need to be.

KHALED   Maybe.

SARAH   No, no maybe.

KHALED   –

SARAH   If she's telling you to quit then perhaps she doesn't
          get it.

KHALED   Get what?

SARAH   What you said, they need people like you.

KHALED   People like who?

SARAH   People who care. People who are going to do
          a proper job.

KHALED   How do you know I'd do a proper job?

SARAH   Because I know a good person when I see one. And
          the fucking optics, remember?

KHALED   –

SARAH   Do you want to be out there?

KHALED   Yes.

SARAH   Do you think you can make a difference?

KHALED   Yes.

SARAH   So…

KHALED   So what?

SARAH   So it matters.

KHALED   Do you think you can make a difference?

SARAH   I hope so.

KHALED   More than me or less than me?

SARAH   I don't understand.

KHALED   –

SARAH   I think that you're uniquely positioned to…

KHALED   Uniquely positioned?

           A beat.

           Why do you want me to stay?

SARAH   Because I think you would regret leaving.
           Because I would like to be with you when we're
           out there.

KHALED   Do you ever speak about me?

SARAH   What?

KHALED   To your friends. Do you mention me?

SARAH   Sometimes.

KHALED   What do you say?

SARAH   That there's this guy I like.

KHALED   That's all?

SARAH   Yes.

           A beat.

KHALED   Do you speak to your parents about me?

SARAH   It's been a week.

KHALED   But do you?

SARAH   Why are you asking me that?

KHALED   It's a question.

SARAH   About my parents.

KHALED   Yes.

SARAH   Okay. Well.
           No, I haven't mentioned you to my mum because
           that would be pretty fucking weird behaviour.

KHALED   –

SARAH   I think you might be getting a little overwhelmed
           by everything at the moment.

KHALED   Actually, do you mind giving me some space?

SARAH   Excuse me?

KHALED   I'm saying I want some space.

SARAH   And I'm saying you just need to relax.

KHALED   –

SARAH   Khaled.

KHALED   Can you please fuck off right now.

           Pause. SARAH *walks over to the door. Then stops
           and walks back over the* KHALED.

SARAH   Sorry, have I done something wrong?
           Cos you're pushing me away after I've spent this
           whole time carrying every single ounce of your
           emotional baggage, I think I am owed an
           explanation.

KHALED   –

SARAH   No? I didn't have to be there for you but I wanted
           to be so can you tell me what's going on right now?

KHALED   –

SARAH   Just so you know, this is some seriously fucked-up
           behaviour, I don't need this.

KHALED   Then leave.

           Pause.

SARAH   No.

KHALED   No?

           Pause.

SARAH   Do you know where I was the other night?
           My ex had to pick up all his old crap. Twelve years.
           And he'd spent most of the time being pretty
           fucking depressed and I'd spent most of the time
           trying to be…
           And he was a piece of shit to me when he was like
           that. And I was so…
           I could feel it, you know, I thought I'd pretty
           much snap.
           And that means the last thing I'm gonna do is make
           someone else feel like they're about to snap. Do
           you understand?

KHALED   –

SARAH   I don't care if you understand, it's true, I'm not
           abandoning you.

KHALED   –

SARAH   Is that clear? You are vulnerable and confused right
           now, I'm not leaving you Ali.

KHALED   –

SARAH   Fuck. Oh my god, fuck, I didn't mean

KHALED   It's okay.

SARAH   It's not.

KHALED   It's fine.

SARAH   No, it's, it's

KHALED   I like it. When you do that.

SARAH   –

KHALED   I still like it.

            The two look at each other.

                                    *

KHALED   'You are an experienced Medical Provider working
            in a refugee camp. During a recent exchange with
            a Primary Actor you promised something which
            you were unable to deliver. You feel you have let
            this Primary Actor down…'

            *SARAH watches KHALED, who reads from an
            index card.*

            '…and so you decide to apologise in an attempt to
            rebuild trust. This is a Primary Actor with whom
            you have become close. But this Primary Actor is
            also vulnerable and tired, wary of authority figures,
            so when you decide to visit them in their own
            home, they seem different.
            They are stubborn and so you must be gentle
            and clear.
            You must be softly spoken.
            You must listen carefully.
            You must be empathetic.
            You must make sure that this Primary Actor feels
            safe and held and needed.'

            A long pause.

            *And now: SARAH and KHALED are alone in
            a tent in a refugee camp.*

SARAH   Hi

KHALED   –

SARAH   Is this okay?

KHALED   There is still no work.

SARAH   Please don't be angry with me.

            A beat.

KHALED   I wish you had said you were coming.

SARAH   I'm sorry, it was
            It was last-minute.

KHALED   My home is very messy.

SARAH   Honestly, you should see my place.

KHALED   Oh you live in a tent?

SARAH   It's just a normal apartment. In the city.

KHALED   –

SARAH   Listen, Ali

KHALED   The cleaning programme did not want me.

SARAH   I know.

KHALED   You say they will give me work but they lose
            money, they disappear.

SARAH   There are other schemes, I can introduce you to
            more people.

KHALED   Who also disappear.

SARAH   The border's shut, at the moment, there's
            a bottleneck.
            But when more people come, money will come, it's
            a matter of time.

KHALED   Everything is time. And everyone says
            I am too young.
            Too old.
            Too vulnerable.
            Not vulnerable enough.
            No education.
            Too much education.
            Too late.
            Too early.

SARAH   You have to trust it'll work out.

KHALED   I know someone, he cleans apartments. The only
            way to get money, he cleans.

SARAH   Whose apartments?

KHALED   Your colleagues, I believe.

SARAH   They shouldn't be doing that.

KHALED   But you say your apartment is a mess.

SARAH   Right.
Okay.
That would be

KHALED   You promised me work.

SARAH   I know.

KHALED   So I believe you owe me.

SARAH   No, the lesson is not: I owe you.

KHALED   Then what is it?

A beat.

SARAH   You know, I could give you a job but at some point
I'll leave.

KHALED   I know.

SARAH   Which means it's not sustainable, it's a stopgap.

KHALED   My whole life is a stopgap.

SARAH   You shouldn't joke.

KHALED   Why? I do not fit here. No one fits: we are all
wrong pieces of a jigsaw, smashed together.

SARAH   –

KHALED   Someone else, she is given medicine, she sells it.
We can do that.

SARAH   That's not happening.

KHALED   So I clean. Little money is all.

SARAH   I can't.

KHALED   Please.

SARAH   You don't need the money.

KHALED   I do.

SARAH   For what? Why exactly do you need money?

KHALED   I need the money because my father is alive.

            Pause.

            Do you believe me?

SARAH   –

KHALED   Someone arrived yesterday.
            They say they see a man – just like him – on the
            border.

SARAH   –

KHALED   You don't believe me.

SARAH   I think it's very unlikely.

KHALED   But I can pay someone to look. It is the only way
            until the border opens.

SARAH   He died.

KHALED   Maybe not.

SARAH   He died and this is not a good idea, Khaled.

KHALED   Ali. Who has a father. Who is alive.

            Pause.

            I am asking because I trust you.
            Or you can leave.

SARAH   –

KHALED   If you are here for yourself and not for me then
            leave.

SARAH   I can't pay you to clean.

KHALED   Then leave.

SARAH   –

KHALED   I understand this game, these rich westerners:
            arrive, leave, arrive, leave.

SARAH   –

KHALED   I do not blame you for being the same, Laura.

SARAH   Don't.

KHALED   No one has to know.

SARAH   –

KHALED   You travel all this way but you cannot do this one thing.

SARAH   A few dollars each time, that's it.

KHALED   Ten.

SARAH   But this – us – it does not exist.

Now NICKI *is there.*

You come and go without me knowing, I will give you a key, I will show you where, I will leave money on the side. Clean once a week – is there a day that works?

KHALED   Any day.

SARAH   Wednesday. Early afternoon.

KHALED   Fine.

SARAH   And if the border reopens, it's over.

NICKI   What's going on?

Pause.

SARAH   Sorry.

NICKI   What is going on?

SARAH   I don't…

The group are back in the room.
SARAH *doesn't have an answer.*

Obviously that was… but

NICKI   But what?

SARAH   –

NICKI   Why are you discussing his father?

KHALED   He needs the border to be open.

NICKI   Excuse me?

SARAH   There are more important things, we need to get the
          border open.

NICKI   Sarah.

KHALED   Listen to her.

NICKI   –

SARAH   My name is Laura, I'm from the organisation, I'm
          asking you to open the border.

NICKI   –

SARAH   These are people fleeing civil war, they're injured,
          they're dying and you're keeping them in tents,
          stuck on the border with nothing. No resources, no
          aid, they need to come here.

NICKI   I'm aware.

SARAH   But are you listening? Are you?

NICKI   I can't do anything here.

SARAH   Yes you can.
          You are in charge of this thing, you can help us.

NICKI   –

SARAH   Do you understand?

          And now: NICKI *and* SARAH *are in a small office
          in a government building.*

NICKI   Those people are not our problem.

SARAH   Yes they are.

NICKI   There are extremist factions amongst them.

SARAH   You know that's not true.

NICKI   Weapons-makers, jihadists.
          And, even if there is no fighting, we will be
          swarmed: thousands of people.

SARAH   You could have let them in slowly.

NICKI   We don't want more of them, that's it.

SARAH   I can't accept that.

NICKI   Then you can go up to them yourself. Use your jeeps.

SARAH   We don't have permission.

NICKI   So it's too scary? You want to save lives but not if
           it's too scary?

           Pause.

SARAH   We have footage of what it's like up there.
           People who haven't eaten in weeks, they look
           hollow.
           There are wounds turning infectious.
           There is disease that is very easy for us to treat.
           Flies feeding on human blood.
           Excrement piled up.

NICKI   You have footage.

SARAH   We sent someone.

NICKI   Show me.

SARAH   When we release it. To the media. And that would
           be a very, very bad look.

           A beat.

NICKI   We can let some through.

SARAH   It needs to be all.

NICKI   It's too many, they'll be fighting for resources.

SARAH   We can build facilities.

NICKI   More of your facilities?

SARAH   As many as we need.

NICKI   No.

SARAH   Why? We have the resources, we can make it better.

           NICKI *scoffs.*

NICKI   You will make us better?

SARAH   That's not what I'm saying.

NICKI   We are your project, we are here for you to fix?

SARAH   That's not what we do.

NICKI   I know your types: coming into countries, we'll
             make it better, don't worry, have a lollipop.
             Not us.
             We are rich, we are proper, we have money.

SARAH   Then use it.

NICKI   We build hospitals.

SARAH   Those hospitals are collapsing.

NICKI   Because they are only built for our people.
             But now there are extra people and our people, they
             complain.
             They say: *The refugees, why do they have better
             hospitals?*
             They say: *The refugees, why do they get food, why
             do they take my job?*
             They say: *Why do they take my land?*
             They say: *We are angry.*

SARAH   So you want us to do nothing.

NICKI   You should take them back with you.

             Pause. And SARAH *is about to leave when –*

             It would need to be worth it. If I do something,
             I need to know it is worth it.

SARAH   I promise it will be.

             Then a phone rings.

NICKI   If we open the border, you build a medical facility
             in the camp, is that right?

SARAH   Yes.

NICKI   For every medical facility in the camp, you build
             one in the city, for our people.

SARAH   Which means you do need our help.

NICKI   Do you agree to the terms?

The phone rings again.

I can make the call. Today. And the border opens.

And again.

I'm sorry, I need to

SARAH   I agree to the terms.

NICKI *answers her phone.*

And now: everyone is there, in the room, watching her.

NICKI   Hello?

    –

    –

My name is Nicola, yes, I'm the sister.

    –

    –

Uh-huh. Right.

    –

    –

Thank you.

She hangs up.

DAN   Is everything…

NICKI   It's fine.

SARAH   Should we keep going?

NICKI   Uh-huh.

SARAH   From where we were or…

NICKI   Actually, who's got the time?

DAN   Just gone four.

            Pause.

NICKI   That was, um, an ambulance picking up my sister
            because of this pain in her…

            NICKI *goes over to her bag, starts packing it –*

DAN   I'm really sorry.

            – and then turns to leave.

SARAH   Is it serious?

NICKI   Excuse me?

SARAH   Is she in danger – like right now?

NICKI   She's stable.

SARAH   Okay.

DAN   Laura.

SARAH   Because you're aware people are moving over the
            border.

            A beat.

NICKI   No, I'm sorry, I can't.

SARAH   It's open. People are flooding across. I don't know
            what other language to use.

NICKI   –

SARAH   There aren't enough tents, no food, water's running
            scarce, security's a nightmare, they keep fighting
            over space.

NICKI   You asked for it to be open.

SARAH   People piling up in the corridors.
            Barely enough staff.
            Look, we're trying to coordinate something here
            and you're

DAN   Can you leave her alone?

SARAH   Me?

DAN   I just think you need to back down.

NICKI   I don't need defending.

SARAH   We're trying to get on with a job can you let us do
          it properly?

DAN   Properly?

SARAH   As in without you getting in the way.

DAN   Oh I'm in the way?

SARAH   Yes.

DAN   I'm an annoyance to you?

SARAH   Yes.

DAN   But what you do is absolutely fine?

SARAH   What I do?

DAN   All the shit you get up to when everyone's back is
          turned.

          And now: SARAH *and* DAN *are in a makeshift
          office in a refugee camp.*

          It's hot, stuffy, cramped.

SARAH   Sorry, what is this?

DAN   –

SARAH   What are you saying?

DAN   It's all in the report, I am simply presenting the
          evidence.

SARAH   There is no evidence.

DAN   I've been told he goes to your flat.

SARAH   By who?

DAN   –

SARAH   He doesn't come to my flat.

DAN   He cleans it.

SARAH	–
DAN	Is that right?
SARAH	No.
DAN	Don't lie to me.
SARAH	–
DAN	You need to be telling the truth right about now.
SARAH	I'm sorry but I think there are more pressing matters.
DAN	I am your manager, I decide what matters.
SARAH	There's a whole influx of people, staff shortages.
DAN	I decide what matters.
SARAH	Charles.
DAN	No, we're not on first-name terms.
SARAH	–
DAN	If this is happening, I need to deal with it.
SARAH	I can't at the moment.
DAN	Why not?

SARAH *doesn't answer. And now* KHALED *is there.* DAN *notices him.*

Is that him?

KHALED	I can go.
SARAH	No. Please. Tell me.
KHALED	Has my father come through?
SARAH	I haven't seen him.
DAN	His father?
SARAH	I don't know.
KHALED	They couldn't find him.
SARAH	That's okay.

KHALED   Has he been registered?

DAN   Laura, this needs to stop

SARAH   Just give me a moment.
         We'll keep looking, okay?

KHALED   I want to go searching.

SARAH   It's getting too violent in the camp.

DAN   Laura.

SARAH   And I can't have you out there, I can't

DAN   LAURA.

SARAH   Fuck.

DAN   –

SARAH   I don't know what to do.

DAN   Can we finish our conversation?

SARAH   Not now.

DAN   Excuse me?

SARAH   Ali, go outside, wait for me.

DAN   No, don't ignore me.

SARAH   I said not now.

         And now: SARAH *and* KHALED *are in modern apartment in the city.*

         It is quiet. Some money is on a table.

KHALED   It feels odd. Normally I am here alone.

SARAH   –

KHALED   I prefer it with you.

SARAH   –

KHALED   Is there a problem?

SARAH   There are records kept. Of everyone who comes
         into the camp. And I looked for your father but

KHALED   There are still more coming.

SARAH   From different places. If he was there then...
          Look, I think it's better you hear the truth and that
          you hear it from me.

KHALED   –

SARAH   I really tried, alright?

KHALED   Maybe I should go.

SARAH   You don't have to.

          A beat. And KHALED *is about to leave when –*

          You should know I'm being threatened by my
          organisation.
          For letting you clean my apartment.
          You didn't even take all of the money I left.

KHALED   I had enough.

SARAH   Well now they might send me home.
          We're having 'a chat' first thing in the morning and
          then I think I'm gone.

KHALED   –

SARAH   I was going to ask if you could speak on my behalf.

KHALED   To say what?

SARAH   You could say that you made me hire you. To clean.
          Or you manipulated me.

KHALED   What?

SARAH   Like how you begged me.
          And the situation with your father.
          And if you told them that, really directly.
          Told them you got on your knees and I had no
          choice.
          Because we're short on people and they might
          just...

          Pause.

          Or maybe I should just quit before they fire me.

KHALED   Okay.

SARAH   You'll do it?

KHALED   If we keep searching.

SARAH   No, that's not

KHALED   Why?

SARAH   I can't pretend that it might be true.

KHALED   But if he is.

SARAH   If he is. Ali. He's gone. Everything else is a fantasy.

KHALED   Don't say that.

SARAH   I know what it's like.
I had dreams about my father.
I was so young, I'd go off to the park, I'd come
home and tell Mum I'd spent the afternoon playing
with him.
These silly games and Mum, she looked horrified,
she had to
She had to tell me so many times.
Your father is dead, your father is dead.

KHALED   Is that true?

SARAH   Yes.

KHALED   Is it?

SARAH   Yes.

KHALED   You're not lying to me?

SARAH   No.

KHALED   Sarah.

SARAH   Laura.

KHALED   Tell me the actual truth.

SARAH   My father is dead.

KHALED   Is he actually?

SARAH   He is dead.

KHALED   In reality, he is actually dead?

SARAH   Yes.

KHALED   Promise me.

SARAH   I promise

KHALED   –

SARAH   I'm sorry but I can't help you search.

KHALED   I will say it was all you.

SARAH   Okay.

KHALED   I will say you forced me.

SARAH   Fine.

Pause. SARAH *approaches* KHALED.

You don't believe that, do you? That I forced you. Please look at me.

SARAH *puts her hands on* KHALED*'s shoulders, then she holds his face.*

I want to stay but you have to accept he's gone.

KHALED   –

SARAH   You poor thing. I wish I could just

Then KHALED *tries to kiss* SARAH. *And* SARAH *pushes him back.*

No, we can't. Do that.

KHALED   Why?

SARAH   –

KHALED   Do you like it?

SARAH   –

KHALED   I like it. I liked it before. I still like it.

SARAH   You're vulnerable right now. Do you understand?

KHALED   No.

SARAH   You're classed as vulnerable, you're a vulnerable
           person.

KHALED   I am 'classed'. You believe this?

SARAH   Of course.

KHALED   No, don't fix me, treat me like a human.

SARAH   –

KHALED   Standing here.
           Look.
           A real adult human.
           With real adult wants.

SARAH   I can't.

KHALED   One of those wants is you.

           SARAH steps back, KHALED steps forward.

SARAH   You should go.

KHALED   I said one of those wants is you.

SARAH   I should go.

KHALED   Do you want to?

SARAH   –

KHALED   Because I don't want anything else.

           Now KHALED kisses her.

           SARAH keeps her hands by her side.

           *Then, after a while, SARAH lifts up her hands and
           clutches KHALED's face.*

           Then they take off each other's clothes.

           They have sex.

           *It's clammy and passionate and awkward and
           tender.*

           And then it's over.

           The two lie there, next to each other, side by side.

           After a while, they seem to be asleep.

Then KHALED *wakes, suddenly and out of breath.*

He tries to calm himself.

He looks at SARAH *who's still asleep.*

Then, slowly, KHALED *gets up and gets dressed.*

He starts to leave.

As he does, SARAH *stirs.*

SARAH   Where are you going?

KHALED   Go back to sleep.

SARAH   What's the time?

KHALED   It's early, you should rest.

SARAH   Khaled?

KHALED   –

SARAH   What is it?

SARAH *stands, looks at* KHALED.

I really enjoyed
all that.

KHALED   Me too.

SARAH   So where are you going?

KHALED   I'm so sorry.

SARAH   For what? Khaled.

KHALED   No.
No.
I went looking for him.

SARAH   What do you mean?

KHALED   Because but I had to see.
In the crowds arriving.
And there were so many
People starving and frantic and pushing, so
crowded that I didn't see.
Someone had a knife.

All of a sudden, KHALED *is bleeding.*

SARAH   Oh my god.

KHALED   I'm sorry.

SARAH   When you said you don't want anything else.

KHALED   I thought I'd find him. I really thought

          KHALED *tries to stay standing but it's difficult.*

SARAH   You're going to be okay. Listen to me, you're
          going to be okay.

          But KHALED *falls over.* SARAH *rushes over to
          him, tries to stem the flow of blood.*

          I need medical supplies NOW.
          You're going to be okay.
          Do you understand?
          I need help NOW.

          DAN *enters.*

          Bandages, gloves, gauze, whatever you can find.

DAN   There's no time, we need to leave.

SARAH   No, get me what I need.

DAN   It's all been taken.

SARAH   What?

DAN   There's no supples, they're looting what they
          can find.

SARAH   I don't understand.

DAN   Everyone else has gone, it's not safe for us. I heard
          gunshots, okay?

          A beat.

SARAH   Ali. Listen to me. Two hands. Firm pressure on the
          wound.

          KHALED *tries to cover the wound. Meanwhile,*
          SARAH *stands and confronts* DAN.

          We can't abandon him.

DAN   Why not?

SARAH   Look at him.

DAN   There are men who've come across the border, they've brought guns.

SARAH   They won't harm us.

DAN   They've already raided our supplies.

SARAH   So find me whatever's left.

DAN   There's nothing.

SARAH   What?

DAN   It is gone and I cannot put you in danger.

SARAH   So bring him with us.

DAN   There's no space.

SARAH   Then find security, find another doctor.

DAN   There isn't anyone.

           A beat.

SARAH   How are you doing Ali?

KHALED   I don't know.

SARAH   Just keep up the pressure.

KHALED   I don't know what I'm doing.

SARAH   Stay calm. Breathe slowly.

           But KHALED's breath is shallow, he's terrified.

DAN   I'm sorry, I don't know what else to tell you.

           Then SARAH goes back to KHALED, places her hands on top of his, on top of the wound.

SARAH   Try to stem the flow. I will come back.

           Then SARAH stands, turns to go –

KHALED   No, don't leave.

           – but then she hesitates—

DAN   We're going now.

SARAH   Give me a moment.

DAN   You need to hurry it up

SARAH   Okay, just, just give me

            – *and still* SARAH *hesitates.*

            DAN *leaves.*

            SARAH *rushes back over to* KHALED, *places her hands on top of his.*

            We're going to be okay. I swear. You are going to be okay.

KHALED   –

SARAH   Say it to me: you're going to be okay.

KHALED   –

SARAH   Say it: you're going to be okay.

KHALED   –

SARAH   Say it.

KHALED   –

SARAH   Say it, tell me, *I am going to be okay*, tell me that right now. Tell me.

KHALED   I'm not.

            SARAH *looks at him.*

            She pauses.

SARAH   What?

KHALED   It's okay, I'm not.

            Then, slowly, she removes her hands.

            KHALED *looks down at the wound, looks up at* SARAH.

            I feel quite weak.

And cold.
And scared.
And tired.
And
Like my eyesight's fading and the world's just a bit
out of reach.

SARAH   Don't be stupid.

KHALED   Can you just
Sorry, I just
Oh look at that, that's a lot of blood.
I had so many
There are so many things when you're young and
you imagine
Just forever
You imagine it's just forever
Watching TV.
On mute.
The news.
The music.
The sunlight mapping across the room.
Into the evening.
Drinking coffee.
Laughing.
Shouting.
Arguing.
In Arabic.
Speaking Arabic.
Speaking to him in Arabic.
Eating sweets.
Telling jokes.
The smell.
The beads.
The clicking.
The clicking.
I can't hear much any more.

SARAH   It's okay.

KHALED   I can't hear it at all.

SARAH   –

KHALED   Can you lie next to me?

           SARAH *does so.*

           And can you
           Like that.

           SARAH *puts her arm around him.*

           Just your breath on my neck. The warmth of it.

           And KHALED *curls up into a ball.*

           Silence.

           And now: the two are back in the room.

           It's late, after the day is over. KHALED *might still
           have some bloodstains on his clothes.* SARAH *is
           still spooning him.*

SARAH   Do you want to go home?

KHALED   Mm-hm.

SARAH   Do you want me to come with you?

KHALED   Mm-hm.

SARAH   Do you want me to stay with you?

KHALED   –

SARAH   I don't have to.

KHALED   I think I want my mum to hug me.

           Pause. SARAH *laughs.*

           What?

SARAH   I knew you were a mummy's boy.

KHALED   Stop it.

SARAH   You're such a mummy's boy. You are, I knew it,
           I fucking knew it!

           SARAH *tickles* KHALED.

KHALED   Stop, alright I'm a mummy's boy, stop!

           SARAH *stops. The two look at each other.*

SARAH   Do you think you should sleep on it?

KHALED   –

SARAH   Just if you regret it.

KHALED   Then I'll regret it.

SARAH   –

KHALED   What?

SARAH   Nothing.

KHALED   What is it?

SARAH   –

KHALED   I'm seeing you Saturday.

SARAH   –

KHALED   I will see you Saturday.

SARAH   Okay.

                              *

            The room is how it was at the start.

            NICKI *enters, with a small bag over her shoulder,
            she puts it in the corner.*

            Soon after, DAN *comes in.*

DAN   Morning.

NICKI   Hey.

            DAN *dumps his bag. Then he drags a couple of
            chairs over to the centre.*

DAN   Um. How's your…

NICKI   She'll be there for a while.

DAN   I'm sorry.

NICKI   They're finding her a carer.

DAN   That's great.

NICKI   No it means she's not doing well.

DAN   –

NICKI   Do you need a hand?

DAN   I'm alright.

           DAN *finishes setting up four chairs, in a sort of semicircle.*

NICKI   Friday.

DAN   Mm-hm.

NICKI   Any plans?

DAN   Not really.
           You?

NICKI   I have no idea what to do with an empty weekend.

DAN   –

NICKI   You wouldn't want to
           If you've got time.
           You wouldn't want to grab a coffee?

DAN   Oh.

NICKI   As in to talk through management things.

           A beat.

DAN   Thank you.

           Then SARAH *enters.*

SARAH   I thought I'd be so late.

NICKI   It's alright.

SARAH   Morning.

DAN   Hey.

           DAN *takes a seat, so does* SARAH.

           Meanwhile NICKI *goes over to her bag, gets out some sheets.*

NICKI   How are we for time?

DAN   Nine fifty-nine.

NICKI   Perfecto.

             Then NICKI *turns back to face the semicircle. She stops for a moment.*

             And, um, Khaled, is he…

SARAH   He's at home.

NICKI   –

SARAH   As in he's
             thinking.
             As in
             he probably isn't coming back.

SARAH   Right. Okay.

DAN   What at all?

SARAH   No.

DAN   Seriously?

NICKI   That's fine.
             Let's just

             A beat.

             NICKI *takes a breath.*
             She takes a seat.

             I think we should start.

             Except no one says anything.
             And there is a blackout.

             The End.

A Nick Hern Book

Multiple Casualty Incident first published in Great Britain in 2024 as a paperback original by Nick Hern Books Limited, The Glasshouse, 49a Goldhawk Road, London W12 8QP, in association with The Yard Theatre, London

Multiple Casualty Incident copyright © 2024 Sami Ibrahim

Sami Ibrahim has asserted his moral right to be identified as the author of this work

Cover image: concept: Kia Nokes; photography: Camilla Greenwell

Designed and typeset by Nick Hern Books, London
Printed in the UK by Mimeo Ltd, Huntingdon, Cambridgeshire PE29 6XX

A CIP catalogue record for this book is available from the British Library

ISBN 978 1 83904 323 9

www.nickhernbooks.co.uk/environmental-policy

www.nickhernbooks.co.uk

facebook.com/nickhernbooks

twitter.com/nickhernbooks